P9-EKS-544

War and Peace Literature for Children and Young Adults: A Resource Guide to Significant Issues

by Virginia A. Walter

ORYX PRESS
1993

The rare Arabian Oryx is believed to have inspired the myth of the unicorn. This desert antelope became virtually extinct in the early 1960s. At that time several groups of international conservationists arranged to have 9 animals sent to the Phoenix Zoo to be the nucleus of a captive breeding herd. Today the Oryx population is nearly 800, and over 400 have been returned to reserves in the Middle East.

Copyright © 1993 by The Oryx Press
4041 North Central at Indian School Road
Phoenix, Arizona 85012-3397

Published simultaneously in Canada

Printed and Bound in the United States of America

♾ The paper used in this publication meets the minimum requirements of American National Standard for Information Science—Permanence of Paper for Printed Library Materials, ANSI Z39.48, 1984.

Library of Congress Cataloging-in-Publication Data
Walter, Virginia A.
  War and peace literature for children and young adults : a resource guide to significant issues / by
Virginia A. Walter.
    p.   cm.
  Includes indexes.
  ISBN 0-89774-725-9
  1. War—Juvenile literature. 2. Peace—Juvenile literature.
I. Title.
U21.2.W3445 1993   92-29729
303.6'6—dc20   CIP

Dedicated to Vivian
and all the grandchildren to come,
with my hope that your generation will never know war.

Contents

Introduction

Why This Book Now?

In 1991, Americans were mesmerized by a war being fought by American soldiers in a desert many had trouble locating on a map. Parents and teachers reported that children showed many signs of anxiety and stress. It was the first war most American children had ever known first-hand. It was the first war in which American mothers went off to fight alongside fathers, leaving some children with both parents away at war. We learned that 65,000 American soldiers were single parents and that parents who were deployed to the Gulf War were required to have alternate-care plans in place in case of their absence or death (Kantrowitz and Mason 1990). It was the first war that most American children watched on television. Peter Jennings even hosted a Saturday morning special just for children, to explain things to them (Rosenberg 1991). Many experts warned that the incessant television coverage would only arouse children's anxieties (Brazelton 1991; Lifton 1991). Researchers at Purdue University found that the antiseptic television coverage of "surgical strikes" left children with the impression that war had been all rockets and no casualties; children evidently didn't associate this war with death ("War Isn't Hell" 1991). *The Wall Street Journal* reported that makers of war toys were positioning themselves for big profits from model planes and Persian Gulf trading cards (Pereia 1991).

In 1990, Americans had also been spellbound as a public television documentary replayed the Civil War in eight installments, using photographs, writings, and music of the time to tell the story. Other wars are less remembered, but significant anniversaries periodically focus media attention on them as well. Thus, the tenth anniversary of the end of the Vietnam War and the fiftieth anniversary of the bombing of Pearl Harbor brought renewed interest in those wars and school assignments to many children.

The short history of the United States is filled with wars. Beginning its nationhood with a bloody Revolutionary War that lasted eight years, the United States has experienced other devastating wars that have helped define its national character. The war with Mexico, from 1846 to 1848, was an offensive war fought under the banner of Manifest Destiny. The Civil War's significance in shaping regional differences, racial tensions, and political values cannot be overestimated. The Indian wars continued until government troops had nearly eliminated the Indian nations that originally occupied this land. The Spanish-American War gave us yellow journalism, Teddy Roosevelt's Rough Riders, and the beginning of a long entanglement with the Philippines. World War I ended American isolationism and, ironically, for the "war to end all wars," set the stage for World War II. The Vietnam War divided our country as no event had since the Civil War. Its legacy lives on in embittered veterans, posttraumatic stress syndrome, and thousands of Vietnamese refugees trying to make new lives in this country.

When I started this book, Americans were at war in the Persian Gulf. As I finish it a year later, we are at peace. Even the Cold War has been declared over. While I cherish the hope that peace will last, I see evidence in current events, as well as in history, that this is unlikely. President Bush has made official pronouncements about going back to the Persian Gulf and "finishing the job," presumably by eliminating Saddam Hussein. Little wars are still being fought all over the globe—in Azerbaijan, Yugoslavia, Sri Lanka, Mozambique. These little wars are devastating to the civilian population, producing economic and social chaos. One result of these local wars is a global phenomenon: refugees seeking haven from the war or political unrest in their home countries. In a 1990 congressional hearing, Dr. Michael Toole, from the International Health Programs Office of the Centers for Disease Control, testified that there were 30 million refugees and displaced persons in the world, victims of war, civil violence, and political persecution, who were dependent on external relief for all their needs. Of these, 20 percent were children under the age of 5; 50 percent were less than 15 years old. Between 13.5 and 15 million children were, at that time, displaced from their homes by war (*Children of War* 1990, p. 19). Many of those refugees end up living in the United States. This may be reason enough to justify a book about children's literature that deals with issues of war and peace.

The urgency of the nuclear threat may have eased with the evaporation of the Cold War. But nuclear weapons are still held by five major powers, and there are constant speculations about who will next join the nuclear club. As long as nuclear weapons exist, children will worry about them.

This book is for adults who care about children living in the frightening, complex society that is the United States in the 1990s, or about children living anywhere in our ever-shrinking world. It presents children's books as the means for creating frames of reference for shared meanings, as sources of information, as starting points for dialogue about the topics of war and peace.

Adults frequently find it difficult to talk to the children in their care about issues that are important in the adult world, about things that really matter. The awkwardness parents have about communicating the facts of life is proverbial, of course, but there are other topics which present equal difficulties: death, religion, violence, injustice, racism, evil, war. What these subjects have in common is a high level of abstraction and an ideological weight. Even the most articulate and caring adult may struggle to find the right words to convey to a four-year-old what it means that grandmother has died or why nigger is a bad word. What is the child capable of understanding? How much truth should one tell? What is the child's frame of reference? In this quest for shared meaning, children's books can sometimes provide the language and the frame of reference.

This book suggests ways that children's books can create frames of reference about the related topics of war and peace. It suggests ways that books can be used to start a dialogue between adults and children, to facilitate communication about a subject that has caused much anxiety in children in this last half of the twentieth century.

The object of this book is not bibliotherapy, as it is ordinarily understood. Trained therapists do use children's books to facilitate insights in their patients, and many of the books discussed in this volume would lend themselves to that use. However, formal bibliotherapy, drawing on both psychoanalytic and learning theories, is a three-step process. Pardeck and Pardeck (1984, pp. 2-3) describe this process as beginning with identification and projection; the reader identifies with a character in a book whose problem is similar to his or her own. The second step involves abreaction and catharsis, in which the therapist supports the reader through an emotional release. Finally, with the therapist's guidance, the reader experiences insight and integration, seeing possible solutions to the problem.

The adults to which this book is addressed, however, are more likely to be teachers, librarians, or parents than therapists. This book is not intended to help laypeople practice bibliotherapy with children, but rather to help adults help children understand the complex issues involved in war and peace. Books are used to create a shared frame of reference and to extend the child's experiences beyond his or her own everyday world. They make abstract or historical concepts more concrete and comprehensible. The Revolutionary War becomes more than a vague reference on the Fourth of July to a seven-year-old who has read *Sam the Minuteman* by Nathaniel Benchley (1969) or to the ten-year-old who has read *This Time, Tempe Wick?* by Patricia Lee Gauch (1974). A twelve-year-old boy who is pondering the meaning of heroism and courage and wondering if he could measure up if tested might find some answers in *Charley Skedaddle* by Patricia Beatty (1987) or *The Boys' War* by Jim Murphy (1990). Books provide children with language and constructs that will help them to understand and to articulate their remaining questions. Books like *All Those Secrets of the World* by Jane Yolen (1991) or *Cecil's Story* by George Ella Lyon (1991), for example, could help young children express their own fears about a parent's absence during wartime. The adult need not be a trained therapist to facilitate this process; the adult need only know the child and the books.

The librarian will recognize this more limited approach as being similar to readers' advisory, or reading guidance, one of the services provided by professional librarians. Unlike reference work, which ordinarily involves the provision of answers to specific questions, reading guidance is the attempt to supply a book which meets a more general or ambiguous need. Librarians often get requests addressing such a need.

"I need to read a novel about the Civil War for my social studies class."

"My four-year-old is always getting into trouble for fighting at nursery school. Do you have any books that will help him see the value of solving problems peacefully?"

"My six-year-old keeps asking me what an atom bomb is. How can I explain it to her?"

"I'm preparing a thematic unit about Japan for my fourth grade class, and I'd like to include information about Japan's role in World War II. What books would you suggest?"

"I'm concerned about the 'Japan-bashing' that is going on now. I'd like my seventh grade students to have some historical perspective. Do you have any books about the experiences of Japanese-Americans in the internment camps during World War II?"

"My five-year-old is obsessed with guns and play soldiers. I need some help knowing how to deal with war toys."

"During the Persian Gulf War, my nine-year-old daughter was fascinated with the idea that women could be soldiers. Do you have any books about women soldiers in the past?"

"Because our elementary school serves a large military base, many of the children had parents who served in the Gulf War. The children still seem anxious about that experience. Do you have any books that would help them deal with their feelings?"

Mae Benne notes that much reading guidance performed by children's librarians is for parents or other adults on behalf of children, rather than directly for children (Benne 1991, p. 84). This book is designed to help adults, as a kind of readers' advisor, to find appropriate children's books that will answer these more general and ambiguous kinds of information needs.

How This Book is Organized

Chapter 1 presents a historical perspective on the process of sharing books about war and peace with children, as well as some of the developmental issues involved with giving the right book to the right child at the right time. Chapter 2 suggests specific techniques for sharing books about war and peace in the library, the classroom, and at home. Chapter 3 presents an analytical overview of the topics of war and peace in children's literature.

The longest part of the book is the classified bibliography, which is divided into the following segments:

Remembering Other Wars: Real and Imaginary
  Stories for Young Children
  Novels for Children
  Fiction for Young Adults
  Nonfiction
Learning about Peace and Conflict Resolution
  Stories for Young Children
  Fiction for Children and Young Adults
  Nonfiction
Timeless Truths from Folk and Fairy Tales
The Vision of Poets
Resources for Adults
  War and Peace
  Parenting, Teaching, Guiding
  Children's Literature

Many of the 480 titles listed in the bibliography are out of print, but all should be readily available in libraries. The bibliography includes books published through 1991. I read every book included in the bibliography, and every title was available in local public or academic libraries or in bookstores. I attempted to be comprehensive in my coverage of fiction, whereas nonfiction titles were added more selectively. Nonfiction titles in the bibliography are either books of unusual quality, books which help to explain some of the events or phenomena presented in the novels, or books on topics not adequately covered in novels. I have included, for example, virtually all of the books for young people about the Holocaust that I could find because this subject is so complex. I wanted all perspectives presented.

Each bibliography entry is accompanied by an annotation that is descriptive and, in many cases, evaluative as well. The annotations are intended to give the reader an idea of both the content and the possible use of the book with children. Books are arranged alphabetically by author.

A word needs to be said about the assigned grade levels. The "Stories for Young Children" sections cover preschool through grade two. "Novels for Children" includes grades three to six. "Fiction for Young Adults" lists titles for grades seven and up. With a couple of exceptions, only novels written and published especially for young adults are included. This eliminates adult novels such as *The Red Badge of Courage* by Stephen Crane or *In Country* by Bobbie Mason, both of which are often read by young people. In all cases, a title is placed in the section for the youngest child that it might interest. In other words, a novel intended for a child in grades five through eight will be found in the "Novels for Children" section, not under "Fiction for Young Adults." In any case, the grade levels are estimates only, based on both the reading level and the reading interest of the presumed reader.

The bibliography is followed by two appendixes containing a literature web and an activity web (see page 22 for a discussion of webbing), and by author, title, subject, and general indexes.

Acknowledgments

I would like to acknowledge the assistance of many dedicated people in helping me identify and locate appropriate books for inclusion in the bibliography, in particular: Judy Kantor, librarian at the UCLA University Elementary School; Susan Patron and Renny Day from the Los Angeles Public Library; Michele Wellck and Kathleen Wheatley, my graduate research assistants at the UCLA Graduate School of Library and Information Science; and Nancy Schimmel, writer, storyteller, and peace activist from Berkeley, California.

References

Benne, Mae. (1991). *Principles of Children's Services in Public Libraries.* Chicago: American Library Association.

Brazelton, T. Berry. (1991, February 25). "What Parents Need to Say." *Newsweek,* 52.

Children of War: Victims of Conflict and Dislocation. (1990). Hearing before the Subcommittee on Children, Family, Drugs, and Alcoholism of the Committee on Labor and Human Resources, United States Senate. One Hundred First Congress, Second Session. April 3, 1990. Washington, DC: United States Government Printing Office.

Kantrowitz, Barbara, and Mike Mason. (1990, November 12). "The Soldier-Parent Dilemma." *Newsweek,* 84.

Lifton, Robert Jay. (1991, February 3). "Parents: To Children, Danger Isn't Distant; It's in the Television." *Los Angeles Times,* M1; M8.

Pardeck, Jean A., and John T. Pardeck. (1984). *Young People with Problems: A Guide to Bibliotherapy.* New York: Greenwood.

Pereia, Joseph. (1991, January 31). "War-Toy Makers Mobilize as Sales Rise." *The Wall Street Journal,* B1; B3.

Rosenberg, Howard. (1991, January 27). "Special War Coverage Turns Kid Time into Prime Time." *Los Angeles Times,* A11.

"War Isn't Hell." (1991, December 9). *Newsweek,* 6.

Children's Books Cited

Beatty, Patricia. (1987). *Charley Skedaddle.* New York: Morrow.

Benchley, Nathaniel. (1969). *Sam the Minuteman.* New York: Harper & Row.

Gauch, Patricia Lee. (1974). *This Time, Tempe Wick?* New York: Coward, McCann, & Geogehegan.

Lyon, George Ella. (1991). *Cecil's Story.* New York: Orchard.

Murphy, Jim. (1990). *The Boys' War: Confederate and Union Soldiers Talk About the Civil War.* New York: Clarion.

Yolen, Jane. (1991). *All Those Secrets of the World.* Boston: Little, Brown.

Chapter 1
The Right Book for the Right Child at the Right Time

Providing the right book for the right child at the right time is one of the traditional objectives of children's librarians as well as one of the purposes of this book. While the bibliography section gives information about a wide range of children's books dealing both specifically and generally with the topics of war and peace, this chapter provides guidance in making the decision in terms of the child, taking into account his or her stage of development and social situation.

A Historical Perspective

In late December 1942, just one year after the United States officially entered World War II, the *New Yorker* noted the publication of *Our Children Face War* by Anna W.M. Wolf. The short review notes that the author ". . . offers sound, quiet counsel, based on experience, on the best methods of adjusting our children to a wartime environment. A boon for worried parents" (p. 60).

Wolf's words of sound, quiet counsel are worth reconsidering 50 years later. She urges mothers to be especially attentive to the needs of their infants and small children, preferring flexibility to rigid training. She urges that children be given simple directions about safety and simple explanations about the nature of war, including death and killing. "Though his life should be free from a constant burden of war talk and emotionalizing, attempts to exclude the war completely or to exert a strict censorship on conversation or other channels of information are usually futile and produce more anxiety than is prevented" (Wolf 1942, p. 33). Children who have been separated from close friends and relatives by the war should be encouraged to participate in all kinds of activities, including but not limited to those involved with fighting and guns. "Children should be permitted to talk freely about the war and its dangers, and parents who can answer their questions honestly can be of great help" (p. 34). The home atmosphere should be kept calm; but if sorrow, death, and disaster intrude, the child should be allowed to share in the grief. Wolf notes that children who are chronically anxious in wartime are probably anxious in peacetime as well. On the other hand, self-confident children will face the war with the same spirit.

Reading Anna Wolf's prescriptions for parents 50 years later, I wondered if those mothers went to their local libraries in 1942 in search of books written for children that would help them provide those simple explanations about war, death, and killing. Another expert on child development, Dorothy W. Baruch, also wrote a book of parental advice in 1942. She acknowledged that telling children where soldiers go was a fact of life as problematical for parents to deal with in the 1940s as telling children where babies come from was in the 1920s (Baruch 1942, p. 23). She appeared to recognize some of the dilemmas that thoughtful parents face when trying to guide their children in difficult times, talking, for example, about the need for children to separate their hatred for the government of Germany from a hatred of the German people (p. 144).

In 1943, an expert on children's reading raised similar concerns. Writing in the *Horn Book*, Bertha Mahoney worried that some American citizens, presumably the Japanese-Americans who were being incarcerated in internment camps, were being persecuted in ways more appropriate to the enemies we were fighting than compatible with our own democratic ideals. She went on to extol an author-illustrator who created books based on two convictions:

> . . . one, the necessity of mutual respect and understanding between people of different nationalities if we are ever to live at peace on this planet; and two, that a big theme may be comprehended by children if it is presented in a way that holds their interest and engages their sympathies. (Mahoney 1943, p. 203)

Ironically, the author Mahoney is referring to is Lucy Fitch Perkins, whose "twins" books are now considered examples of patronizing, ethnocentric children's books about other cultures that contribute to the reinforcement of stereotypes rather than to true understanding. However, the point was still made that children's books are an appropriate vehicle for facilitating understanding of complex issues and for developing values.

Certainly publishers have responded with books designed to meet a demand for material about war, death, and killing, if not always to facilitate respect and understanding between nations. Browsing through the issues of *Horn Book* that were produced during World War II, one finds many telling examples. In 1943, the David McKay Company announced its list of 11 Christmas gift books for children. Of these, six are war-related, including *Corporal Crow* by Margaret Friskey, a book for four- to eight-year-olds about "Inky, a soldier crow, who saves the farmer's corn from the Japanese beetles, much to the surprise of old colonel crow who promotes him to corporal" (Advertisement for *Corporal Crow, Horn Book,* 1943). Not all of the books published during this period were about World War II, of course; but the influence of that war shows in many of the children's books that we still have on our library shelves today. Esther Forbes won the Newbery Medal for excellence in children's literature in 1943 for *Johnny Tremain.* In her acceptance speech, she makes clear that she saw many connections between her novel about the American Revolution and the war that was being fought as she wrote. She contrasts the occupation of Boston by British troops with the occupation of European cities by the Nazis.

> The boys and girls of the age I made Johnny Tremain were reading of the treatment Norwegians, Dutchmen, Poles, and Frenchmen were enduring under the Nazis. . . . It seemed to me that too often our schools have held up the British redcoats as ogres. From everything I could read of the period, it seemed to me that their occupation of Boston from 1774 to 1776 was as humane a military rule as anyone could possibly imagine. . . . And I really wanted young people today to think of the British in Boston—and the Nazis in, say, Rotterdam. (Forbes 1944, pp. 266-67)

Forbes goes on to make her purpose even clearer:

> In peace times countries are apt to look upon their boys under twenty as mere children and (for better or worse) to treat them as such. When war comes, these boys are suddenly asked to play their part as men. Our young fliers today have much in common with the nineteen-year-old boys who served as captains of armed ships during the Revolution. Their rank did not depend on how old they might be, but how good. It was true then as now. . . .
>
> I also wanted to show that these earlier boys were conscious of what they were fighting for and that it was something which they believed was worth more than their own lives. And to show that many of the issues at stake in this war are the same as in the earlier one. We are still fighting for simple things "that a man may stand up." (Forbes 1944, p. 267)

Presumably adults put both *Corporal Crow* and *Johnny Tremain* in the hands of children because they seemed like the right books for those children at the time, books which would help them to understand war, as Anna Wolf had advised. *Johnny Tremain* also happened to be a work of considerable literary merit and outlived both the time of its publication and any didactic or ideological purpose the author might have had in writing it. *Corporal Crow*, on the other hand, is long out of print, having little relevance or value after the war was over.

In retrospect, at least, World War II does not appear to have caused the agony of ideological conflict for the American people than some other wars have. There appears to have been a considerable consensus that it was a just war, fought against aggressors who could not be stopped by any other means. Both the books of parental advice and the books written for children about war at the time seem to be aimed at bolstering a child's patriotism and courage in the face of adversity. Children's books are cultural artifacts, after all, reflecting the times in which they are written. Adults should have little difficulty finding the right book for the right child at the right time if they select books written at the time—providing the adult agrees with the prevailing dominant ideology.

A study conducted during the Vietnam War found that children of that era accepted the necessity and even the inevitability of war. The researcher found that strong messages about patriotism were communicated to children by both parents and schools even during that relatively unpopular war, and the children appeared to mirror the dominant value of their society. It is interesting, however, that black children were more likely to oppose American involvement in the Vietnam War than white children were (Tolley 1973). This may reflect the cynicism of lower status groups about the values of the dominant culture.

Fifteen years later, attitudes and concerns about the Vietnam War had changed considerably, and so had the approach of educators, as the contributors to a special issue of *Social Education* indicate. In that issue, W.D. Ehrhart points out: "Each generation only knows what the previous generations are willing to teach it, and very little has been taught about Vietnam" (1988, p. 26). In the absence of any formal teaching, he notes that young people's knowledge about Vietnam has largely been informed by mass media images, such as the Sylvester Stallone movie character Rambo. Fred Wilcox (1988) also worries about the ahistorical bias of young people and the difficulty of making contemporary adolescents understand either the cynicism of many members of the Vietnam generation or the idealism and traumatic loss of faith which so many Vietnam veterans exemplify.

During the Persian Gulf War, the newspapers were full of advice to parents, and several children's books were rushed to press to meet the presumed information needs of children and their caregivers. This was another war which seemed to be overwhelmingly supported by the American people. The advice given by the experts in child development sounded eerily similar to that given during World War II. Dr. Lee Salk responded to a mother who wondered how to help her five- and six-year-old boys, who became both curious and agitated when they watched television reports about American soldiers in Saudi Arabia:

> Encourage your boys to ask questions, and give them honest answers. . . . Certainly you can say that war is a terrible thing, yet we still need to have young men and women ready to defend national principles, and that the President, the United Nations and other countries always try to solve problems without fighting. (Salk 1991)

While most books published during the Persian Gulf War were for older children, *Only Soldiers Go to War* by Lucinda Kennaley (1991) might have been written just to help a parent follow Dr. Salk's advice. It is an uncritical, simple explanation of how the United States got involved in the Persian Gulf War.

Many experts addressed the problem of separation from their soldier parents that confronted children during the Persian Gulf War. Fred Rogers, the beloved Mr. Rogers of public television, produced media spots designed to soothe children's fears; child psychologist Miriam Winikoff recommended that caregivers help children create a treasure box filled with letters, gifts, and videos from their absent parents (Ansberry and Hymowitz 1991). *"My Desert Storm" Workbook* (1991), produced by the National Childhood Grief Institute, was designed to help children both confront and soothe their fears about war and separation. Also published in 1991 were two picture books about other wars which dealt with a young child's fears about an absent soldier father: *All Those Secrets of the World* by Jane Yolen, a nostalgic look back at World War II, and *Cecil's Story* by George Ella Lyon, set during the Civil War. Were these authors motivated, as Esther Forbes was, by current events?

Parents who were opposed to the war in the Persian Gulf would have had a hard time finding books to share with their young children that represented their point of view. They would have had to look back to some of the books published during the Vietnam War to find more general anti-war messages. A revisionist view of the Persian Gulf War has yet to appear in books for children.

Some Developmental Issues

In addition to the ideological content of children's books about war and peace, adults sharing these books with children will also want to consider the child's developmental and reading levels. These are not the same issues. A book may be written at a second or third grade level and have the appearance of a picture book for a young child and still have a content that is appropriate for a much older child.

Let the Celebrations Begin! by Margaret Wild (1991) and *My Hiroshima* by Junko Morimoto (1990) are good examples. Both have the large print and simple sentences that we associate with texts for beginning readers. Both are lavishly illustrated with childlike pictures and presented in a typical picture book format. Yet the subject matter is extremely problematical in each. *Let the Celebrations Begin!* is a story about children in Nazi concentration camps and *My Hiroshima* is about the bombing and destruction of Hiroshima. The horror of both events has eluded most adults who try to comprehend it. How much more difficult would it be for the very young child for whom these books seem by their appearance to be intended? How many young children would even choose, of their own volition, to read about either the Holocaust or Hiroshima? Few young children under the age of nine or ten would have the historical frame of reference or the cognitive development or the emotional maturity to adequately deal with the issues raised by either of these books. If the parent of a much younger child had a good reason to introduce the subject of the Holocaust or the bombing of Hiroshima, however, these books could be used with sensitive adult intervention. The key is adult intervention. Young children would surely have questions after looking at the pictures of naked, burned bodies in *My Hiroshima*; they deserve to have caring adults nearby to answer those questions.

If one is truly going to find the right book for the right child at the right time, it is necessary to know both the child and the book—and to be there at the right time. There are some general developmental guidelines that one can follow.

Phyllis La Farge, a former editor of *Parents* magazine, relates the broad developmental stages of childhood to children's concepts of war and peace. She points out that four- and five-year-olds think in very concrete, egocentric terms and have little information about the world outside the family. They pick up knowledge about war from the society around them—primarily from the media and from family members, often accurately interpreting the tone in which the information is presented (or concealed). Seven- and eight-year-olds are still quite concrete in their cognitive patterns, but the differences between boys and girls begin to be more obvious. Boys focus on the artifacts of war—weapons and military equipment. Girls are more likely to worry about fighting, dying, and killing. Nine- and ten-year-olds have a personal response to war and peace, thinking in terms of "making friends" or "making up." With their strong focus on peer relations, they worry about lingering conflicts. Young adolescents, the twelve- to fourteen-year-olds, bring a concern about the future to their worries about war. They may be obsessed with the threat of nuclear disaster and respond with a feeling of meaninglessness and helplessness, or a sense that life is out of control. They may also feel angry that they could be robbed of their future by nuclear war (La Farge 1987, pp. 46-60).

Sybille Escalona is a psychiatrist who has done extensive research on children's fears about nuclear war. In a pamphlet prepared for parents by the Child Study Association of America, she made similar observations about the needs of children at different ages, as they relate to their concerns about nuclear war (Escalona 1962). She notes that four- to six-year-olds are easily frightened by noise and violence because they are struggling with noisy, violent emotions themselves. Parents can help by protecting and reassuring, limiting their explanations, avoiding overstimulation, clearing up misunderstandings, and sharing values that support reason and dignity in the conduct of human affairs. Middle childhood, the period from six to twelve, is less characterized by fearfulness in general, but children at the upper end of this age span may worry that they won't be strong enough to deal with a nuclear war. They know more about the world and their place in it, so their fears are quite realistic. They cope with their fears best by acquiring knowledge and mastery and living on the borrowed strength of caring adults. Parents can help by encouraging open conversation, continuing to clear up misunderstandings, emphasizing positive steps that can be taken to counteract the dangers of nuclear war, and communicating attitudes and values that support friendly relations among nations. Adolescents are concerned with the future, with their own future in particular. They may respond to the nuclear threat by rejecting all adult values and authority, by denying the existence of the threat, by adopting a *carpe diem* approach to life, or, optimally, by seeing the threat as a spur to maturity. Parents can help by affirming the independence of their teenage children, providing opportunities for constructive exploration away from home, and remembering that their influence is stronger than it may appear.

Some child development experts make the case that it is not enough to consider cognitive and emotional development when transacting information with children. The specific life experiences of the child are also important. James Garbarino and his colleagues at the Erikson Institute in Chicago have developed a model for understanding what goes on when an adult and a child are communicating in an effort to exchange information. The model presents two dimensions of the communication context: orientation and competence.

The child's performance in the communication process depends partly on his or her orientation to the situation. Both psychological and sociocultural factors affect the child's orientation. Psychological factors might include wanting to please the adult or, conversely, being afraid of the adult or being distrustful of the adult's motives or authority. Sociocultural factors would include the child's culture, values, and lifestyle. Middle-class children, for example, learn that adults sometimes ask children questions in order to find out whether the child knows the right answer. Children from lower socio-economic groups, particularly urban African-American children, assume that when an adult asks a question, it is because the adult wants to know the answer. The child's competence depends largely on levels of cognitive and language development such as those we have been discussing.

The adult's orientation depends on the role he or she is playing in the information transaction. Social workers, teachers, librarians, and parents all play different roles as they exchange information with children. The role tends to influence motives, expectations, and attitudes. Imagine the different motives and expectations that a teacher, a police officer, and a social worker might have in asking a 10-year-old child, "Do you know what a bomb is?" The adult's competence is related to skill in analyzing the child's status on the two dimensions and in creating a situation that will enable the child to perform optimally (Garbarino 1989, pp. 15-17).

Garbarino and his associates have developed this model primarily for social workers and psychologists, but it is relevant to teachers and librarians and most adults who interact with children in an information-giving or information-seeking mode. For example, we will be looking at the different modes for sharing literature with children that arise from the different adult roles of teacher, librarian, and parent in the next chapter. Adults should be aware of the roles they adopt when exchanging information with children, the child's orientation to the situation in which the information exchange is taking place, and the child's relative competence in giving and getting information. For our purposes, we would probably also want to add knowledge of children's literature as a factor affecting the adult's competence in guiding the information exchange to an effective conclusion.

The objective of this book, of course, is to help the adult to match an individual child, at a particular stage of development and emerging from a particular sociocultural context, with the right book, the book that will meet the child's expressed need to know or the adult's desire to facilitate the child's understanding and knowledge in the particular subject domain of war and peace. Some of the research on children's responses to literature is helpful here.

Children's Responses to Literature

Arthur Applebee (1978, pp. 123-125) has related children's responses to literature to Jean Piaget's formulation of the stages of cognitive development in children. He finds that children in Piaget's preoperational stage (ages two to six) respond verbally to literature by narrating or retelling the story, without a real sense of the overall plot, but rather as a series of incidents. They experience the story as it unfolds and are unable to develop a coherent, integrated response. A five-year-old may focus on one detail of a narrative, such as Peter Rabbit's lost jacket, instead of seeing or remembering the whole story. In the concrete operational stage (ages seven to eleven), they are able to summarize and categorize their responses. They can usually tell what a story is about and what they think about it. At the beginning of the formal operational stage (ages twelve to fifteen), children are able to analyze both the structure of a literary work and the motives of characters. They are also able to identify self-consciously with the text. This is a significant leap; they are able to separate subjective responses to literature from the objective nature of the work itself. Older children can handle more ambiguity in a story.

Bruno Bettelheim (1975) has claimed that children's subjective responses to one form of literature—the folk tale—may be more important than their objective responses. The objective response to a fairy tale is delight and enchantment, important in itself, and is a response to the literary or aesthetic qualities of the story. The subjective responses, however, serve an important psychoanalytic function by helping children deal with their unconscious feelings, including their dark side. They convey meaning about the most important aspects of human existence, the conflicts between good and evil, and they do this almost entirely at an unconscious or subjective level. Bettelheim writes: "Fairy tales enrich the child's life and give it an enchanted quality just because he does not quite know how the stories have worked their wonder on him" (p. 19).

Research done in a broad range of disciplines—cognitive science, child development, psychiatry, education—shows that children will respond most effectively to books with content, tone, perspective, scope, and language that are appropriate to both their level of development and life experience. I don't want to overstate this. Professionals who work a great deal with children and books have observed that children will frequently skip over passages in a book that they don't understand. In most cases, children are not harmed by being exposed to a book that is too "mature" or too "difficult." Children are very good at finding their own level of involvement with a text. However, some of the themes and subjects found in the books listed in this bibliography are particularly sensitive, for the adult who is sharing the book if not for the child. The younger the child, the more critical this is likely to be. Particularly if the adult's intent in sharing a book is to communicate a particular value or point of view, one would want to be sure that the book was likely to evoke the desired response. Selecting such books for children is as much an art as a science, but some general guidelines and cautions can be drawn.

1. Adults should read the book before sharing it with children. Use the annotations in this bibliography or elsewhere as guidelines for initial selection, but don't rely on them. You need to have first-hand knowledge of the book as well.

2. Do not rely on the format of the book to indicate the appropriate age of the reader. Remember the picture books discussed earlier, *Let the Celebrations Begin!* and *My Hiroshima*, which are intended for much older children than the usual picture book audience.

3. Remember that children under the age of five are very egocentric and very concrete in their thinking. Books about war should be reassuring and take into consideration the child's frame of reference. Children at this age know very little about the world; books can widen their knowledge of the world but should do so in a context that builds on the child's own experiences. Books about peace need to be concrete; abstract concepts of harmony and resolution are not comprehensible to young children.

4. Children from the ages of six to nine still cannot dependably separate reality from fantasy on television, in books, or in their lives. Fears and anxieties tend to be very strong at this age. As Bettelheim pointed out, fairy tales may help them deal with some of their fears at the subconscious level where the fears are strongest. Books may help children at this age articulate their anxieties and start a dialogue with adults, who can then help them understand

what's real and reassure them about their fears. Family stories and realistic stories about children like themselves are good choices for this age.

5. Children from ten to twelve are particularly receptive to information that will give them mastery over an uncertain world. Information can be very empowering to them. Their knowledge and experience of the world is more sophisticated, and they are better able to integrate fantasy into their cognitive maps without being confused about whether or not it is "real." Their historical and geographical perspectives should be developed enough to enable them to absorb stories about events that are remote from their own experiences. They should have the rudimentary critical thinking skills that will enable them to evaluate information as well.

6. Young adolescents, thirteen and over, are concerned with issues of identity. They relate well to books in which characters are testing themselves against difficult obstacles. They are also idealistic and concerned about moral and ethical issues of war and peace. Their metacognitive skills are well-developed; they can think about thinking and separate their own responses from the objective nature of a text. Unfortunately, sometimes their reading level is not equal to their cognitive or interest level. The more sophisticated picture books on this list—*The Butter Battle Book* by Doctor Seuss (1984), *Hiroshima No Pika* by Toshi Maruki (1980), *Faithful Elephants* by Yukio Tsuchiya (1988), or *Rose Blanche* by Roberto Innocenti and Christophe Gallaz (1990)—might be perfect for starting discussions about ethical issues of war with teenagers who are less fluent readers.

7. Avoid being too literal in thinking about the subjects of war and peace in literature for children. Most children's books about war are also about peace, at least implicitly. Peace must be taught in a broader context than simply peace. Katherine Paterson has made the point most eloquently that children need words of comfort and images of compassion in order to grow towards peace. From her perspective, the best books to give a young child who is anxious about war might be *Goodnight Moon* by Margaret Wise Brown (1947), with its comforting cadence and cozy, intimate, predictable world view, or *Crow Boy* by Taro Yashima (1955), with its message of compassion. Paterson writes: "We are not wise enough, we adults, to know what book will be right for any child at any particular moment, but the richer the book, the more imaginative

the language, the better the chance that it will minister to a child's deep, inarticulate fears." (Paterson, 1991, p. 34)

Paterson's references to literary quality are also relevant to the question of a child's response to any book. Some of the titles listed in this bibliography have little merit beyond their objective content or didactic purpose, and I suspect that children's responses to these books will be weak. If a novel fails to engage the young reader, through a compelling plot, vivid language, and interesting characters, it does not matter that the subtext or message was correct. If the illustrations in a picture book are static or contrived, young children are unlikely to linger over them. Children may not detect bias or misinformation in a nonfiction work, but they will notice awkward writing or a condescending tone. While literary merit is not a dimension that has been researched as a factor in children's responses to literature, it makes sense, as Paterson pointed out, that children will instinctively respond more deeply to what is fine than to what is shoddy.

Sensitive Topics

Two topics require more extended discussion. The issues of nuclear war or nuclear fear and the Jewish Holocaust are particularly sensitive to most children and to many adults. Both topics carry a heavy ideological and emotional weight. Both nuclear war and the Holocaust have been targets of controversy at various times in educational, political, and religious communities. Adults need to think carefully about how they want to present these subjects to children.

Nuclear War

The threat of nuclear war is one that even well-informed, sophisticated adults have difficulty comprehending and integrating into their world views. It is impossible to calculate the probability of its occurrence, in spite of the best efforts of military defense strategists. The consequences are unimaginable and yet all-encompassing, affecting all living people and their children and their children's children.

The immediacy of the nuclear threat ebbs and flows with the international political situation for most of us. Sybille Escalona (1982) found that children's concerns about nuclear war reflect the attitudes and values of adults around them. Thus, at the time she was writing her article, she found that nuclear war was not a foreground concern for children, but she asserted that it could become one when a crisis situation arose. Even so, she found that knowledge of the possibility of nuclear disaster permeates our society and affects our view of the world and our place in it.

Children respond with sensitivity to anything that is surrounded by a feeling of the uncanny and mysterious—a feeling such as that attached to our thoughts of nuclear disaster. The catastrophes of which we have experience are limited in time and space. In our lifetime millions have been killed in war and millions of Jews were slaughtered, and these events did leave their mark. But the thought that virtually all people in a huge area might suddenly die and sicken, and that survivors would have no life supports, leaves us with the prospect of something like a black hole or a vacuum. The fact, well understood by many children, that plants, water, and all organic life can at the same time be destroyed, touches upon deep and primitive fantasies of world destruction. (p. 605)

Escalona's conclusions are also worth quoting in some detail:

To the extent that the present functioning of society conveys to children a picture of passive and evasive withdrawal, of fear of and belligerence toward other nations, and of not even trying to combat a host of evils both large and small—to that extent the effects of the nuclear peril upon us also affects the development of children. The adult response to ultimate danger, is, to growing children, also the ultimate test of the trustworthiness of adult society. (p. 607)

The implications of such ideas for parents, caregivers, and professionals working with children are sobering. William Beardslee and John Mack (1983), two child psychiatrists who have studied the issue extensively, advise parents and other adults who must help children deal with their nuclear fears to confront their own fears first. Acknowledge the pain and horror that you feel. Then consider carefully the child's developmental level and cognitive ability to think about the future. Young children, under the age of eight or nine, will need reassurance more than information. Finally, Beardslee and Mack suggest that the adult try to find out directly what specific concerns the child has before offering information or counsel. Children vary greatly both in the nature of their concerns and the quality and quantity of information they have about the nuclear threat.

As Escalona predicted in 1982, crisis situations have brought about renewed concern about nuclear war. The Persian Gulf War brought with it a resurgence of reports of children's fears and adult insecurity about dealing with them. Responding very quickly, Charlotte Wallinga (1991) and her colleagues in the Department of Child and Family Development at the University of Georgia summarized the research and listed a number of implications for classroom teachers. Like Beardslee and Mack, they advised teachers to address their own feelings about nuclear war and to seek out supportive resources. They warned that teachers should be prepared for controversy, that parents may be concerned that the topic is too frightening or that the teacher's political position is different from their own. They reminded teachers that children need to discuss their feelings as well as the more objective questions of fact.

Teachers who want to address the issue of nuclear war in the classroom should indeed be prepared for controversy. They should be aware of any state and local policies governing nuclear education. Some nuclear education curricula have been criticized as being too frightening (Adelson & Finn 1985) or too "liberal" (London 1987). Educators who decide to proceed with a nuclear curriculum will find useful resources in the Wallinga article cited above. A more general approach to peace education is described in some detail in *Educating for Global Responsibility*, edited by Betty Reardon (1988).

While thinking about the threat of nuclear war, we should not forget that nuclear weapons have been used in the past and that the United States was the nation that used them. Some adults have found it useful to refer to that historic event as a jumping-off point for talking with children about the possibility of another nuclear war. Japanese children learn about the bombing of Hiroshima and Nagasaki earlier than American children do, and they are not spared the horror of the effects of the bombings on ordinary people (Hotta 1991). Surely American children have as much reason and need to know. Many of the books on this list provide a place to start. I have already mentioned the two picture books, *Hiroshima No Pika* and *My Hiroshima*. In spite of their picture format, the graphic illustrations make these more suitable for older children. *Sadako and the Thousand Paper Cranes* by Eleanor Coerr (1977) is a particularly good choice for children in fourth or fifth grade; Sadako's courage and her indomitable desire for peace make her an accessible heroine, rather than simply a victim. Adults should be prepared for the inevitable question: "Why did the United States government decide to use the bomb?" Books like *Looking the Tiger in the Eye* by Carl Feldbaum and Ronald Bee (1985) will help formulate the answer.

The Holocaust

The systematic extermination of the Jewish people in Europe by the Nazi government during World War II presents similar problems for adults who are confronted with the need to explain this event to children. We call it the Holocaust, although it is in fact unnameable. We say it is unimaginable, although it was imagined and implemented by real human beings as a matter of government policy. To confront the facts of the Holocaust is to confront evil and its consequences. As adults, we are repelled by the amorality and inhumanity of its perpetrators and appalled by the horrors suffered by its victims. How can we communicate any of this to children in ways that they can understand? Some adults have recommended that we not even try. The issue is controversial, particularly in the Jewish community. After all, if the truth is more than a child can bear, how much more traumatic might it be for a Jewish child? Jewish children must assimilate the fact that hundreds of thousands of children were killed in Europe just 50 years ago for no other reason than that they were Jewish, just like they are. It brings the horror to the very center of a child's identity.

Jewish educators have offered advice over the years. There is general agreement now that, no matter how painful, it is important that children learn the facts about the Holocaust, taking into consideration the child's age and life situation (Derevensky 1988; Posner 1987-1988). There is more danger in ignorance or forgetfulness than in remembering. There is also general agreement that children, particularly young children, should be protected from the more graphic or horrific details. One approach that has worked successfully for some parents is to begin with general information about the Holocaust and add details as the child grows older.

In the next chapter, we will address the question of context as it applies to the general topic of sharing books about war and peace with children. It seems appropriate to say a word here about some of the different settings in which one might share books about the Holocaust. The family is probably the most appropriate setting for learning about the Holocaust. Loving parents can provide both reassurance and appropriate information. Public libraries will want to have a wide range of children's books on the Holocaust to meet the needs of children and their caregivers for information at different levels and for novels that make the Holocaust accessible to contemporary children. Teachers in public schools will probably teach the Holocaust as part of history units on World War II or in literature classes when particular novels are introduced. Jewish educators will probably feel more responsibility for integrating the topic throughout the curriculum. All educators will need to be sensitive to how the particular point of view of the materials they are using relates to the life experiences of the students and the religious values of the parents. Diane Roskies has summarized a number of approaches to Holocaust education that have been used in Jewish schools, finding a wide variety of strategies in use, from an Orthodox affirmation of the working of God in history to a Zionist interpretation of the Holocaust as a predictable end to the collision of cultures caused by the Jewish presence in Europe (Roskies 1975, p. 2). Even the educational objectives to be furthered by teaching the Holocaust have been debated: teaching for knowledge versus teaching for identification (Roskies 1975, p. 6).

Whatever the objective or strategy, adults will find that children's books will be helpful in providing information and establishing a dialogue. Most children's books about the Holocaust protect children from the full horror of the event and most offer an ultimate message of hope. Rachel Meir (1986-1987) writes about some of the ways that authors of children's books about the Holocaust have protected children. Novels tend to isolate specific events relating with the Holocaust, such as a family's escape. More horrible experiences tend to be handled indirectly, as a story told by someone or in a letter or in an overheard conversation. This, of course, raises the related issue of accuracy in children's books about the Holocaust. Freda Kleinburd looked at all children's books about the Holocaust that were written in English or translated into English from the early 1940s through 1986. She was concerned with how the books portrayed Jewish resistance, the survival rate of European Jewry, and non-Jews, as well as with any purely factual errors. More than half of the books she examined accurately conveyed the fact that most Jews in Nazi-occupied Europe were killed. Few books focus on the Jews who died, however; almost all of the protagonists are survivors. She found that the issue of Jewish resistance is handled appropriately. Non-Jewish characters, however, appear to be far less anti-Semitic and more helpful to their Jewish neighbors than the historical record suggests is accurate. Knowing these limitations should help adults as they share books about the Holocaust with children. Roskies (1975) recommends that nonfiction be introduced along with the novels in order to present a more accurate overview.

References

Adelson, Joseph, and Chester E. Finn. (1985, April). "Terrorizing Children." *Commentary*, Vol. 79, No. 4, 29-36.

Advertisement for *Corporal Crow*. (1943). *Horn Book*, Vol. 19, No. 6, 361.

Ansberry, Clark, and Carol Hymowitz. (1991, January 29). "Gulf War Takes a Toll on Soldiers' Children; 'I Want My Momma'." *The Wall Street Journal*, A1; A8.

Applebee, Arthur N. (1978). *The Child's Concept of Story: Ages Two to Seventeen*. Chicago: University of Chicago Press.

Baruch, Dorothy W. (1942). *You, Your Children, and War*. New York: Appleton-Century.

Beardslee, William R., and John E. Mack. (1983). "Adolescents and the Threat of Nuclear War: The Evolution of a Perspective." *The Yale Journal of Biology and Medicine*, Vol. 56, 79-91.

Bettelheim, Bruno. (1975). *The Uses of Enchantment: The Meaning and Importance of Fairy Tales*. New York: Knopf.

Derevensky, Jeffrey L. (1987-1988). "Introducing Children to Holocaust Literature: A Developmental-Psychological Approach." *Judaica Librarianship*, Vol. 4, No. 1, 53-54.

Ehrhart, W.D. (1988). "Why Teach Vietnam?" *Social Education*, Vol. 52, No. 1, 25-26.

Escalona, Sybille. (1962). *Children and the Threat of Nuclear War*. New York: Child Study Association.

———. (1982). "Growing Up with the Threat of Nuclear War: Some Indirect Effects on Personality Development." *American Journal of Orthopsychiatry*, Vol. 52, No. 4, 600-07.

Forbes, Esther. (1944). "The Newbery Medal Acceptance." *Horn Book*, Vol. 20, No. 4, 262-67.

Garbarino, James et al. (1989). *What Children Can Tell Us: Eliciting, Interpreting, and Evaluating Information from Children*. San Francisco: Jossey-Bass.

Hotta, Ann. (1991). Personal conversation with the author.

Kleinburd, Freda. (1989-1990). "Historical Accuracy in Children's Literature of the Holocaust." *Judaica Librarianship*, Vol. 5, No. 1, 57-61; 70.

La Farge, Phyllis. (1987). *The Strangelove Strategy: Children, Parents, and Teachers in the Nuclear Age*. New York: Harper.

London, Herbert I. (1987). *Armageddon in the Classroom: An Examination of Nuclear Education*. Lanham, MD: University Press of America.

Mahoney, Bertha E. (1943). "The World Republic of Childhood." *Horn Book*, Vol. 19, No. 4, 203.

Meir, Rachel. (1986-1987). "Introducing Holocaust Literature to Children." *Judaica Librarianship*, Vol. 3, No. 1-2, 65-67.

Paterson, Katherine. (1991, January/February). "Living in a Peaceful World." *Horn Book*, Vol. 68, No. 1, 32-38.

Posner, Marcia W. (1988). "Echoes of the Shoa: Holocaust Literature—Part I." *School Library Journal*, Vol. 34, No. 1, 36-37.

———. (1988). "Echoes of the Shoa: Holocaust Literature—Part II." *School Library Journal*, Vol. 34, No. 2, 30-31.

Reardon, Betty A., editor. (1988). *Educating for Global Responsibility: Teacher-Designed Curricula for Peace Education, K-12*. New York: Teachers College Press.

"Review" of *Our Children Face War*. (1942, December 26). *New Yorker*, 60.

Roskies, Diane K. (1975). *Teaching the Holocaust to Children: A Review and Bibliography*. KTAV.

Salk, Lee. (1991, February). "Helping Children Understand War." *McCalls*, 40.

Tolley, Howard, Jr. (1973). *Children and War: Political Socialization to International Conflict*. New York: Teachers College Press.

Wallinga, Charlotte et al. (1991). "Children and Nuclear War." *Childhood Education*, Vol. 67, No. 4, 260-63.

Wilcox, Fred A. (1988). "Pedagogical Implications of Teaching 'Literature of the Vietnam War'." *Social Education*, Vol. 52, No. 1, 39-40.

Wolf, Anna W.M. (1942). *Our Children Face War*. Boston: Houghton Mifflin.

Children's Books Cited

Brown, Margaret Wise. (1947). *Goodnight Moon*. New York: Harper & Row.

Coerr, Eleanor. (1977). *Sadako and the Thousand Paper Cranes*. New York: Putnam.

Feldbaum, Carl B., and Ronald J. Bee. (1985). *Looking the Tiger in the Eye: Confronting the Nuclear Threat*. New York: Harper & Row.

Forbes, Esther. (1943). *Johnny Tremain*. Boston: Houghton Mifflin.

Friskey, Margaret. (1943). *Corporal Crow*. New York: McKay.

Innocenti, Roberto, and Christophe Gallaz. (1990). *Rose Blanche*. New York: Stewart, Tabori and Chang.

Kennaley, Lucinda. (1991). *Only Soldiers Go to War*. Springfield, MO: Thoth.

Lyon, George Ella. (1991). *Cecil's Story*. New York: Orchard.

Maruki, Toshi. (1980). *Hiroshima No Pika*. New York: Lothrop.

Morimoto, Junko. (1990). *My Hiroshima*. New York: Viking.

"My Desert Storm" Workbook: First Aid for Feelings. (1991). New York: Workman.

Seuss, Dr. (1984). *The Butter Battle Book*. New York: Random.

Tsuchia, Yukio. (1988). *Faithful Elephants: A True Story of Animals, People and War*. Boston: Houghton Mifflin.

Wild, Margaret. (1991). *Let the Celebrations Begin!* New York: Orchard.

Yashima, Taro. (1955). *Crow Boy*. New York: Viking.

Yolen, Jane. (1991). *All Those Secrets of the World*. Boston: Little, Brown.

Chapter 2
Using Books about War and Peace in the Library, in the Classroom, and at Home

The context in which books about war and peace are introduced to children makes a difference. In this chapter, we will discuss the library, the classroom, and the home as three different settings in which adults might be sharing the books listed in the bibliography with children. In each case, the role of the adult in relation to the child is different. The reasons for sharing the books are different. The ways in which the books are introduced are different. This is a practical, how-to-do it chapter, with an emphasis on ideas and techniques. It is not intended to be prescriptive, but rather to suggest some starting points.

The Library

The librarian's role will vary slightly if the setting is a public library or a school library media center. A public librarian is more likely to be dealing with parents, youth group leaders, and other caregivers, while the school library media instructor is more likely to be dealing with classroom teachers. However, both professionals will be confronted with specific demands for information about war and peace and with the more elusive reading guidance requests. The bibliography should be helpful in both cases.

Professional librarians understand the need to be sensitive when conducting reference interviews that reveal a need for information about war and peace. Some children may have difficulty articulating this need. One librarian told me about a child who asked her for a book that would show her what war looked like. This was in the period before Operation Desert

Shield erupted into Operation Desert Storm. She had seen the pictures of soldiers on television with their tanks and other war materiel, but she couldn't imagine what it would be like if they really started fighting. Books with photographs of Vietnam and World War II battles appeared to satisfy her curiosity. Some adults may have difficulty explaining the context for their request. Do they want to convey a particular point of view or set of values to children? Are they trying to alleviate a child's fears? Provide factual information? Start a dialogue? Librarians may need to keep their own political, philosophical, or religious views to themselves in order to provide the nonthreatening, nonjudgmental, objective, value-neutral assistance their patrons need. Sometimes it may be effective to set up a display of books on this topic and simply let the books speak for themselves.

In addition to providing reference and reading guidance and creating topical displays, librarians are accustomed to promoting books and language development through other activities, most particularly by giving booktalks and storytelling. The following sections show how books about war and peace can be used in those contexts.

Booktalks

Librarians give booktalks to promote books. Booktalks can be short, informal descriptions of books that the librarian shares while doing reading guidance, or they can be fairly formal presentations to groups, in which the librarian talks at some length about one or more books. As Joni Bodart puts it:

> A booktalk is not a book review or a book report or a book analysis. It does not judge the book's merits; it assumes the book is good and goes on from there . . . . A good booktalk reaches out to the listeners and involves them so they become not merely listeners but participants. It makes them care enough about the people in the book to want to read it and see what happens after the end of the talk. (Bodart 1980, p.3)

Frequently, the occasion for a booktalk is a class visit to the library, whether it is the public library or the school library media center. Librarians also frequently give booktalks when they visit classrooms. In either case, the librarian is trying to promote library use by highlighting some of the books in the collection. I like to build a booktalk around a theme that enables me to draw in books from various parts of the collection. Sometimes the theme is provided by a teacher; then I am able to demonstrate that we have books in the library that will be useful for homework purposes. Sometimes I use a theme that enables me to spotlight unusual or interesting books that children might miss otherwise.

Many good coherent booktalks can be built around themes or subjects that are spelled out in the subject index of this book. The bibliography could lead you to booktalks based on the Civil War or refugees, for example. This might be an appropriate response to a teacher's request for books on a specific thematic unit. Another possibility is to start with a book from the bibliography that is exciting and worth introducing to young people and building a theme-based booktalk that includes other books that are not about war or peace. For example, a booktalk for sixth graders about wolves might lead off with Whitley Streiber's *Wolf of Shadows* (1985), go on to *Julie of the Wolves* by Jean Craighead George (1972) and *Wolves* by R.D. Lawrence (1990), and conclude with a sly telling of *The True Story of the Three Little Pigs* by Jon Scieszka (1989), a fairy tale send-up that I have found is most appreciated by older, more sophisticated children. The advantage to this approach is that the books about war and peace are not isolated but are integrated with other books with similar themes. You haven't singled out nuclear war as a subject; it has merely emerged as the backdrop for a powerful story about wolves. This broadens the possible audience for *Wolf of Shadows* and highlights the fact that it is more than a story about nuclear war.

Patrick Jones (1990) suggests a number of ways to present booktalks that will appeal especially to hard-to-reach young adult audiences. He recommends beginning with magazines or music and moving on to movies. Talk about movie tie-ins. You could build a whole booktalk around the movie *Glory*, using *Undying Glory* by Clinton Cox (1991) and *Which Way Freedom?* by Joyce Hansen (1986), as well as other books about black soldiers. Relate personal experiences. I find that young people today are fascinated by my experiences as an anti-war protester in the 1960s; it doesn't seem to matter that these experiences took place more than 25 years ago. Share inside information about the authors or the story behind the story. Jones writes: "When I tell students that Mazer's *The Last Mission* is based on a true story, I can sense that interest in the book increases" (Jones 1990, p. 29).

Here are some other possibilities for booktalks that include titles about war or peace but do not focus on those themes. The books listed in this bibliography are starred.

Walls—for a third grade class
* * Bunting, Eve. *The Wall.*
* * Giblin, James. *Walls: Defenses Throughout History.*
  Lee, Jeanne. *The Legend of the Li River.*
  Mahy, Margaret. *The Seven Chinese Brothers.*

Heroines—for a fourth grade class
* * Gauch, Patricia Lee. *This Time, Tempe Wick?*
* * Langton, Jane. *The Fragile Flag.*
  Lord, Bette Bao. *In the Year of the Boar and Jackie Robinson.*
  Minard, Rosemary. *Womenfolk and Fairy Tales.*
* * Reit, Seymour. *Behind Rebel Lines: The Incredible Story of Emma Edmonds, Civil War Spy.*
  Young, Ed. *Lon Po Po.*

Brothers and Sisters—for a fifth grade class
    Conrad, Pam. *My Daniel.*
    Konigsberg, E.L. *From the Mixed-Up Files of Mrs. Basil E. Frankweiler.*
    Marshall, James. *Hansel and Gretel.*
    Moeri, Louise. *Save Queen of Sheba.*
 * Pearson, Kit. *The Sky Is Falling.*

Survival (or Islands)— for a sixth grade class
    Cole, Brock. *The Goats.*
    Defoe, Daniel. *Robinson Crusoe.*
 * Degens, T. *Game on Thatcher Island.*
 * Orlev, Uri. *The Island on Bird Street.*
    Steig, William. *Abel's Island.*

Time Travel—for a sixth grade class
    Eager, Edward. *The Time Garden.*
    L'Engle, Madeleine. *A Wrinkle in Time.*
    Park, Ruth. *Playing Beatie Bow.*
 * Yolen, Jane. *The Devil's Arithmetic.*

Creativity—for a seventh grade class
    Cameron, Eleanor. *A Room Made of Windows.*
    Jarrell, Randall. *The Bat-Poet.*
    Lyons, Mary E. *Sorrow's Kitchen.*
 * Paulsen, Gary. *The Monument.*

Whichever approach you choose to take with booktalks, be sure that you promote books that you have read and that you genuinely like. Working with children in Los Angeles, I have learned to make my booktalks as multicultural as possible and to include a wide range of reading levels.

Storytelling

Librarians tell stories with pictures to young children, and they tell traditional folk tales orally, without the book, letting children form the pictures in their imagination. As with booktalks, there are basically two subject approaches that you could take if you wanted to share books or stories from the bibliography with children. During the Persian Gulf War, for example, it might have been entirely appropriate to build a story time for preschoolers around the theme of soldiers. A story time based on soldiers might still be relevant for Veterans Day or Memorial Day or even the Fourth of July. Possible stories to use are *Drummer Hoff* by Barbara Emberley (1967), *All Those Secrets of the World* by Jane Yolen (1991), *Amifika* by Lucille Clifton (1977), and *Stone Soup* by Marcia Brown (1947). Most of the time you would want to build out to other kinds of picture books and stories as the following examples suggest.

Preschool Story Hour

Giants
* Foreman, Michael. *The Two Giants.*
"Jack and the Bean Stalk."
Seeger, Pete. *Abiyoyo.*

Books and Libraries
Browne, Anthony. *I Like Books.*
Bunting, Eve. *The Wednesday Surprise.*
* De Paola, Tomie. *The Knight and the Dragon.*
Kimmel, Eric. *I Took My Frog to the Library.*

Playing
Ets, Marie Hall. *Play with Me.*
Greenfield, Eloise. *Me and Neesie.*
Henkes, Kevin. *Jessica.*
* Naylor, Phyllis Reynolds. *King of the Playground.*

Traditional Story Hour

I might build a story hour for adults around a theme of peace, but I would hesitate to do so for children. I think it would end up sounding too didactic, without the magic that children associate with storytelling. I do like to use a theme, however loose, as an organizing principle for my story hours; and some of the stories in this bibliography would work nicely with other themes.

Clever Girls
"Clever Manka" in *Womenfolk and Fairy Tales* by Rosemary Minard.
* "I'm Tipingee, You're Tipingee, We're Tipingee Too" in *The Magic Orange Tree and Other Haitian Folktales* by Diane Wolkstein.
Mufaro's Beautiful Daughters by John Steptoe.

How and Why
"Anansi's Hat Shaking Dance" in *The Hat Shaking Dance and Other Anansi Tales* by Harold Courlander.
The Legend of the Milky Way by Jeanne M. Lee.
* "Loo-Wit, the Fire-Keeper" in *Native American Stories* by Joseph Bruchac.

Big and Little
"Billy Beg and the Bull" in *Favorite Fairy Tales Told Around the World* by Virginia Haviland.
The Inch Boy by Junko Morimoto.
* *Once a Mouse . . .* by Marcia Brown.

In addition to using stories as part of formal story hour sessions, it is often effective to tell one story as part of a booktalk or library orientation.

I also like to tell stories spontaneously to small groups of children who are at hand and in the mood for a story.

In the Classroom

Some of the classroom uses of children's books about war and peace are obvious. Books about historical events such as the Revolutionary War or World War II are always relevant to social studies or history classes. The educational movements for a whole language approach to reading and a literature-based curriculum are particularly supportive of the use of novels as a mechanism to teach history. As Lou Willet Stanek (1991, p. 189) puts it: " . . . history is what happened and literature is what people felt about it." I like to pair a novel and a nonfiction title and show young people how they are related. Some good pairs from this list are:

> *After the Dancing Days* by Margaret Rostkowski and *The Trenches* by
> Dorothy and Thomas Hoobler.
> *Charlie Pippin* by Candy Dawson Boyd and *Always to Remember: The
> Story of the Vietnam Veterans Memorial* by Brent Ashabranner.
> *The Father of the Orphans* by Mark Bernheim and *Shadow of the Wall*
> by Christa Laird.
> *The Spring Rider* by John Lawson and *Lincoln: A Photobiography* by
> Russell Freedman.

A closer look at the whole language approach reveals that demonstrating relationships between different books and between books and real life is one of its basic tenets.

Whole Language and the Literature-Based Curriculum

Stanek explains how the whole language approach to reading is based on the concept of integration—integrating the language arts of listening, speaking, writing, and reading; integrating the discipline by taking reading and writing across the curriculum, and integrating the child's experience and the curriculum.

One technique that many classroom teachers are using to demonstrate the integration of reading across disciplines is webbing. Webbing is a way of mapping the linkages that grow out of one book. The linkages may be to a variety of activities or to a variety of other books. Appendix A is an example of a literature web based on *Park's Quest* by Katherine Paterson (1988), appropriate for a sixth or seventh grade class. Appendix B is an example of an activity web based on *Sadako and the Thousand Paper Cranes* by Eleanor Coerr (1977), appropriate for a fourth or fifth grade class. Teachers can present such webs to their students in order to help them develop a systematic reading program or to motivate them to read more by dramatizing the fascinating interconnectedness of literature. Librarians sometimes prepare webs for teachers to help them develop a thematic unit. Kay Vandergrift and Jane Hannigan (1991) point out that students can also participate effectively in webbing activities. They say that the process of webbing invites a deeper look at both context and content, encouraging young people to seek deeper meanings and personal insights.

Reading aloud is another practice endorsed by the whole language movement. I discuss reading aloud in some detail later in this chapter as a technique for parents to share literature with children, but teachers should not ignore its personal and educational rewards either. Episodic novels like *A Blue-Eyed Daisy* by Cynthia Rylant (1985) lend themselves to brief read aloud sessions. Children who have a hard time getting started on *The Search for Delicious* by Natalie Babbitt (1969) may find this novel irresistible when a teacher shares its rich language and sly humor. Reluctant teenage readers may find themselves riveted by the plight of the young parents in Yuri Suhl's *On the Other Side of the Gate* (1975). A unit on the Civil War could spring to life with a reading of *Shades of Gray* by Carolyn Reeder (1989).

Critical Thinking

Another current educational movement is a trend to incorporate critical thinking as an element of teaching across the curriculum. Variously defined, critical thinking is fundamentally a more active form of learning in which students are engaged in questioning the material rather than just receiving information in a rote fashion. The *American Educators' Encyclopedia* (1982, p. 137) defines critical thinking as " . . . the ability to judge and evaluate information and/or evidence, drawing conclusions that are objective and logical." Generally, this ability incorporates a number of core thinking skills, which together comprise critical thinking. Dennis Abrams and Mary Hamm (1990, pp. 40-41) have generated a list of these thinking skills, which should be part of the learning objectives of the elementary curriculum.

1. *Focusing Skills*—attending to selected chunks of information.
2. *Information-gathering Skills*—becoming aware of the substance or content needed.
3. *Remembering Skills*—activities involving information storage and retrieval.
4. *Organizing Skills*—arranging information so that it can be understood or presented more effectively.
5. *Analyzing Skills*—classifying and examining information of components and relationships.
6. *Generating Skills*—using prior knowledge to add information beyond what is known or given.

7. *Integrating Skills*—putting things together, solving, understanding, forming principals.
8. *Evaluating Skills*—assessing the reasonableness and quality of ideas.

Many educators have made a good case for integrating the teaching of these skills into every area of the curriculum. (Clarke 1990; Ruggiero 1988). The topics and specific titles included in this bibliography are particularly appropriate for critical thinking activities in a number of curriculum areas. A science class could look closely at conflicting scientific claims about the possible effects of nuclear winter or Agent Orange. Social studies classes could investigate the Civil War from the point of view of both North and South, using novels from this list. Many of the novels offer rich opportunities for gathering, organizing, analyzing, integrating, and evaluating information. A sixth grade class could read *In the Eye of War* by Margaret and Raymond Chang (1990), for example, and look for internal evidence that Shao-Shao's neighbor has collaborated with the Japanese. This could lead to a discussion of German accommodation to Hitler's policies and the viability of resistance in such cases.

Michelle Commeyras (1989) has suggested that literature is a good vehicle for teaching elementary students some of the critical thinking skills. Her approach involves a close reading of the text and the development of alternative interpretations of a story. Using the example of *In the Eye of War*, the assignment might be to develop alternative scenarios for Shao-Shao. What would have happened if *his* family had been collaborators? How would the story have been different? Could the children have resisted if their parents had been more cooperative with the occupying regime? Do children always adopt the political doctrines and practices of their parents? Why? Older students might read *Road to Memphis* by Mildred Taylor (1990) and discuss what might have happened if Moe had not fought with Statler or if Jeremy had not helped Moe get away.

Literature lends itself to a discussion of moral and ethical values. Susan Resnick Parr (1982) has written about her method of focusing on the moral and values dimension of literature while teaching literature to college students. Many of the questions she raises could also be used with gifted elementary school students or typical junior high and high school students; and they are particularly relevant to novels dealing with themes of war and peace. The following questions raised by Parr as general literary issues are particularly relevant:

1. How much freedom do individuals really have?
2. How much freedom do people really want?
3. What criteria should people use when faced with conflicts between their personal sense of morality and social customs and laws?
4. Are human beings inherently good or inherently evil?

5. How do such factors as race, gender, and class affect individual freedom?

6. What has been the effect of technology on individual freedom?

7. What factors lead people to dehumanize one another? What factors lead to violence? (Parr 1982, pp. 20-22)

Imagine the stimulating classroom discussion that could result from raising these questions about Robert Westall's *The Machine Gunners* (1976), Chester Aaron's *Gideon* (1982), or Myron Levoy's *Alan and Naomi* (1977).

Classroom teachers who want to incorporate critical thinking skills in their teaching will find that their school library media instructors or local librarians are good allies and consultants. Jacqueline Mancall (1986) and her colleagues have developed a model of a school library media program which is built on the objective of educating children to think. Many of the critical thinking skills are also incorporated in the concept of information literacy, which is the focus of much current thinking in the library profession. Given the ideologically charged content of many of the books which deal with war or peace, the need to bring critical thinking skills to them is essential. With their expertise in information resources, librarians can work with teachers and students to identify materials and information strategies which will foster a reflective response.

At Home

Parents share books with their children for many reasons. They want to stimulate a love of reading and encourage the development of strong reading skills. In particular, reading aloud to children brings a number of rewards. For young children, it builds listening and language skills, as well as providing the "literature-rich" environment that many early childhood educators find is necessary for emergent literacy (Morrow 1989; Taylor 1983). By reading aloud, parents build shared frames of reference with their children. Families who read together bring a multitude of literary characters and events into their lives. Madeline, Frog and Toad, Max and the wild things, and Ferdinand the bull will be among the first. Forever after, a reference to "smelling the flowers just quietly" will trigger memories for all of you of the peace-loving bull. Later, Aslan and Marmee, Meg, Jo, Amy, and Beth may join your household, bringing with them a knowledge of the fantasy land of Narnia and nineteenth-century family life that would otherwise be far removed from the everyday lives of you and your children.

Particularly relevant for the subject of this book is the opportunity for communication which family reading aloud can provide. When children are read to, they are able to relate to the reader and respond to ideas that they would not be able to read by themselves. They can ask questions about things they don't understand. From the shared meanings that books provide, parents can also raise questions for discussion and introduce values and concepts that might seem forced or contrived without a grounded context. Peace, for example, is a particularly elusive concept for children to grasp. Evidence suggests that children find war much easier to imagine. Parents who want to talk about peace with their very young children might find *The Story of Ferdinand* by Munro Leaf (1936) a good place to begin. Here is a bull who is expected to fight ferociously but who prefers to sit quietly smelling the flowers. That is peace. *The Two Giants* by Michael Foreman (1967) would be another good choice since it demonstrates the folly of fighting and the ease with which conflict can get out of hand. *Peace Begins with You* by Katherine Scholes (1990) is more direct and didactic but makes its point in a relatively childlike way.

Advocates of the family read-aloud tradition urge that parents continue the practice long after children are able to read for themselves. As Margaret Mary Kimmel and Elizabeth Segal (1988) point out, reading aloud continues to be a rich experience for both parents and children; it's too much fun to stop when the kids learn how to read. Besides, it promotes the child's desire to read independently; it whets the appetite for more. Parents can continue to read books of mutual interest to adult and child but with a reading level beyond the child's capability and can use these as springboards to meaningful dialogue. Many of the novels in this bibliography are rich with conflict and ambiguity that would lend themselves to discussion. Sensitive parents will know, however, when to leave a child alone with his or her thoughts. Some of the most significant responses to literature are private and delicate and easily destroyed by rough handling. It may be enough to just read *Friedrich* by Hans Peter Richter (1970) or *Autumn Street* by Lois Lowry (1980) together and rest quietly with the knowledge that both parent and child have shared a powerful vicarious experience.

There are several good guides to the technique of reading aloud. The Kimmel and Segal book cited above or *The New Read-Aloud Handbook* by Jim Trelease (1989) are good choices if you feel you need more guidance. It is not a very mysterious process. Choose books that you enjoy. As a basic principle, choose books with rich language, vivid characters and events, and a strong narrative line. With a child that you know well, you can alternate those with more introspective books. Select a time when you won't be distracted by other demands. Right after supper or just before bedtime are typical read-aloud times. Use a light hand when exploiting a book for its message; too much didacticism can kill a child's natural response and enjoyment of a book. Books that reflect your own values will communicate those values without your calling attention to them.

References

Abrams, Dennis M., and Mary C. Hamm. (1990). *Cooperative Learning: Collaboration Across the Curriculum*. New York: Charles C. Thomas.

American Educators' Encyclopedia. (1982). Westport, CT: Greenwood.

Bodart, Joni. (1980). *Booktalk! Booktalking and School Visiting for Young Adult Audiences*. New York: H.W. Wilson.

Clarke, John H. (1990). *Patterns of Thinking: Integrating Learning Skills in Content Teaching*. Boston: Allyn and Bacon.

Commeyras, Michelle. (1989). "Using Literature to Teach Critical Thinking." *Journal of Reading*, Vol. 32, No. 8, 703-07.

Jones, Patrick. (1990). "Booktalking Boosters: Eighteen Ideas to Reach Those Under Eighteen." *Emergency Librarian*, Vol. 18, No. 2, 28-30.

Kimmel, Margaret Mary, and Elizabeth Segal. (1988). *For Reading Out Loud! A Guide to Sharing Books with Children*. New York: Delacorte.

Mancall, Jacqueline C., Shirley L. Aaron, and Sue A. Walker. (1986). "Educating Students to Think: The Role of the School Library Media Program." *School Library Media Quarterly*, Vol. 15, No. 1, 18-27.

Morrow, Lesley Mandel. (1989). *Literacy Development in the Early Years: Helping Children Read and Write*. Englewood Cliffs, NJ: Prentice Hall.

Parr, Susan Resneck. (1982). *The Moral of the Story: Literature, Values, and American Education*. New York: Teachers College Press.

Ruggiero, Vincent Ryan. (1988). *Teaching Thinking Across the Curriculum*. New York: Routledge.

Stanek, Lou Willett. (1991). "Whole Language for Whole Kids: An Approach for Using Literature in the Classroom." *School Library Journal*, Vol. 37, No. 9, 187-89.

Taylor, Denny. (1983). *Family Literacy: Young Children Learning to Read and Write*. Portsmouth, NY: Heinemann.

Trelease, Jim. (1989). *The New Read-Aloud Handbook*. New York: Penguin.

Vandergrift, Kay E., and Jane Anne Hannigan. (1991). "Oldies But Goodies: Hidden Treasures from Your Shelves." *School Library Journal*, Vol. 37, No. 9, 174-79.

Children's Books Cited

Aaron, Chester. (1982). *Gideon*. New York: Lippincott.

Ashabranner, Brent. (1988). *Always to Remember: The Story of the Vietnam Veterans Memorial*. New York: Dodd, Mead.

Babbitt, Natalie. (1969). *The Search for Delicious*. New York: Farrar, Straus & Giroux.

Bernheim, Mark. (1989).. *The Father of the Orphans*. New York: Dutton.

Boyd, Candy Dawson. (1987). *Charlie Pippin*. New York: Macmillan.

Brown, Marcia. (1961). *Once a Mouse* . . . New York: Macmillan.

———. (1947). *Stone Soup*. New York: Scribner's.

Browne, Anthony. (1988). *I Like Books*. New York: Knopf.

Bruchac, Joseph. (1991). *Native American Stories*. Golden, CO: Fulcrum.

Bunting, Eve. (1990). *The Wall*. New York: Clarion.

———. (1989). *The Wednesday Surprise*. New York: Clarion.

Cameron, Eleanor. (1971). *A Room Made of Windows*. Boston: Little Brown.

Chang, Margaret, and Raymond Chang. (1990). *In the Eye of War*. New York: McElderry/Macmillan.

Clifton, Lucille. (1977). *Amifika*. New York: Dutton.

Coerr, Eleanor. (1977). *Sadako and the Thousand Paper Cranes*. New York: Putnam.

Cole, Brock. (1987). *The Goats*. New York: Farrar, Straus & Giroux.

Conrad, Pam. (1989). *My Daniel*. New York: Harper & Row

Courlander, Harold. (1957). *The Hat Shaking Dance and Other Ashanti Tales*. New York: Harcourt, Brace and World.

Cox, Clinton. (1991). *Undying Glory: The Story of the Massachusetts 54th Regiment*. New York: Scholastic.

Defoe, Daniel. (1719). *Robinson Crusoe*. New York: Scribner.

Degens, T. (1977). *Game on Thatcher Island*. New York: Viking.

De Paola, Tomie. (1980). *The Knight and the Dragon*. New York: Putnam.

Eager, Edward. (1967). *The Time Garden*. New York: Harcourt Brace Jovanovich.

Emberley, Barbara. (1967). *Drummer Hoff*. New York: Simon & Schuster.

Ets, Marie Hall. (1955). *Play with Me*. New York: Viking.

Foreman, Michael. (1967). *The Two Giants*. New York: Pantheon.

Freedman, Russell. (1987). *Lincoln: A Photobiography*. New York: Clarion.

Gauch, Patricia Lee. (1974). *This Time, Tempe Wick?* Coward, McCann & Geoghegan.

George, Jean Craighead. (1972). *Julie of the Wolves*. New York: Harper & Row.

Giblin, James. (1984). *Walls: Defenses Throughout History*. Boston: Little, Brown.

Greenfield, Eloise. (1975). *Me and Neesie*. New York: Crowell.

Hansen, Joyce. (1986). *Which Way Freedom?* New York: Walker.

Haviland, Virginia. (1985). *Favorite Fairy Tales Told Around the World*. Boston: Little Brown.

Henkes, Kevin. (1989). *Jessica*. New York: Greenwillow.

Hoobler, Dorothy, and Thomas Hoobler. (1978). *The Trenches: Fighting on the Western Front in World War II*. New York: Putnam.

"Jack and the Bean Stalk." (1967). In Joseph Jacobs, *English Fairy Tales*. New York: Dover. (Also available in many other fairy tale collections).

Jarrell, Randall. (1963). *The Bat-Poet*. New York: Macmillan.

Kimmel, Eric. (1990). *I Took My Frog to the Library*. New York: Viking.

Konigsberg, E.L. (1967). *From the Mixed-Up Files of Mrs. Basil E. Frankweiler*. New York: Atheneum.

Laird, Christa. (1989). *Shadow of the Wall*. New York: Greenwillow.

Langton, Jane. (1984). *The Fragile Flag*. New York: Harper & Row.

Lawrence, R.D. (1990). *Wolves*. San Francisco: Sierra Club Books.

Lawson, John. (1968). *The Spring Rider*. Boston: Little, Brown.

Leaf, Munro. (1936). *The Story of Ferdinand*. New York: Viking.

Lee, Jeanne M. (1983). *The Legend of the Li River*. New York: Holt.

———. (1982). *The Legend of the Milky Way*. New York: Holt.

L'Engle, Madeleine. (1962). *A Wrinkle in Time*. New York: Farrar, Straus & Giroux.

Levoy, Myron. (1977). *Alan and Naomi*. New York: Harper & Row.

Lord, Bette Bao. (1984). *In the Year of the Boar and Jackie Robinson*. New York: Harper & Row.

Lowry, Lois. (1980). *Autumn Street*. Boston: Houghton Mifflin.

Lyons, Mary E. (1990). *Sorrow's Kitchen: The Life and Folklore of Zora Neale Hurston*. New York: Scribner.

Mahy, Margaret. (1990). *The Seven Chinese Brothers*. New York: Scholastic.

Marshall, James. (1990). *Hansel and Gretel*. New York: Dial.

Mazer, Harry. (1981). *The Last Mission*. New York: Dell.

Minard, Rosemary. (1975). *Womenfolk and Fairy Tales*. Boston: Houghton Mifflin.

Moeri, Louise. (1981). *Save Queen of Sheba*. New York: Dutton.

Morimoto, Junko. (1986). *The Inch Boy*. New York: Penguin.

Naylor, Phyllis Reynolds. (1991). *King of the Playground*. New York: Atheneum.

Orlev, Uri. (1984). *The Island on Bird Street*. Boston: Houghton Mifflin.

Park, Ruth. (1982). *Playing Beatie Bow*. New York: Atheneum.

Paterson, Katherine. (1988). *Park's Quest*. New York: Dutton.

Paulsen, Gary. (1991). *The Monument*. New York: Delacorte.

Pearson, Kit. (1990). *The Sky Is Falling*. New York: Viking.

Reeder, Carolyn. (1989). *Shades of Gray*. New York: Macmillan.

Reit, Seymour. (1988). *Behind Rebel Lines: The Incredible Story of Emma Edmonds, Civil War Spy*. San Diego: Harcourt Brace Jovanovich.

Richter, Hans Peter. (1970). *Friedrich*. New York: Holt, Rinehart & Winston.

Rostkowski, Margaret I. (1986). *After the Dancing Days*. New York: Harper & Row.

Rylant, Cynthia. (1985). *A Blue-Eyed Daisy*. New York: Bradbury.

Scholes, Katherine. (1990). *Peace Begins with You*. San Francisco: Sierra Club/Boston: Little, Brown.

Scieszka, Jon. (1989). *The True Story of the Three Little Pigs*. New York: Viking Kestrel.

Seeger, Pete. (1986). *Abiyoyo*. New York: Macmillan.

Steig, William. (1976). *Abel's Island*. New York: Farrar, Straus & Giroux.

Steptoe, John. (1987). *Mufaro's Beautiful Daughters: An African Tale*. New York: Lothrop, Lee & Shepard.

Streiber, Whitley. (1985). *Wolf of Shadows*. New York: Knopf.

Suhl, Yuri. (1975). *On the Other Side of the Gate*. New York: Watts.

Taylor, Mildred. (1990). *The Road to Memphis*. New York: Dial.

Westall, Robert. (1976). *The Machine Gunners*. New York: Greenwillow.

Wolkstein, Diane. (1978). *The Magic Orange Tree and Other Haitian Folktales*. New York: Schocken.

Yolen, Jane. (1991). *All Those Secrets of the World*. Boston: Little, Brown.

———. (1988). *The Devil's Arithmetic*. New York: Viking Kestrel.

Young, Ed. (1989). *Lon Po Po*. New York: Philomel.

Chapter 3
A Literary Overview

This chapter will pull together some of the major themes and issues raised in and by the 400 books about war and peace for children and young people that are included in this bibliography. This chapter is both an overview and a preview of the rich content you can expect to find as you begin consulting the bibliography, reading the books, and sharing them with children.

A Backward Look

A backward look at the titles in this bibliography gives us some information about the social forces that may have influenced the authors, editors, and buying public of the time. Children's books are cultural artifacts. As Anne Scott MacLeod puts it:

> Like all literature, they reflect their time and place in a variety of ways, some of them direct, some indirect, some deliberate and intentional on the part of the author, some far less conscious. Like popular literature (which they resemble in several ways), children's books tend to convey conventional views more often than individual idiosyncracy, thus offering insight into the common assumptions, the accepted ideas, and the widely shared opinions of a culture. Above all, of course, children's literature reflects the attitudes toward children and childhood of the society that produces it. (MacLeod 1985, p. 100)

The earliest novel included in this bibliography is Louisa May Alcott's *Little Women*, written in 1868, just after the Civil War. The first half of the novel is framed by the absence of the father who is serving as a chaplain in the war. The story is set in an atmosphere of feminine domestic tranquillity which separates the haven of home from the harsh masculine reality of the battlefield. The conflicts at home are made to appear trivial against the greater conflict being fought elsewhere in the country. Alcott was herself a volunteer nurse with the Union Army until her health gave way, and she may have idealized the harmonies of domestic life to help rationalize that experience. This is one of the few children's classics to survive and be read from the nineteenth century, and its interest for young readers today tends to lie in the more unconventional characters—rebellious Jo and snotty Amy, especially Jo, who would have run away to the war herself if she could.

The only consistency in later children's novels about the Civil War is their pro-Union point of view. Only Patricia Beatty's *Turn Homeward, Hannalee* (1984) and *Be Ever Hopeful, Hannalee* (1988) and Carolyn Reeder's *Shades of Gray* (1989) present the Southern world view with sensitivity. Recent nonfiction, however, has been less biased in its presentation of both sides. Particularly notable is *The Boys' War* by Jim Murphy (1990) which uses historic photos and documents to portray the very young soldiers who fought and died on both sides.

There is a long break in the chronology until the publication of *Gay-Neck* by Mukerji in 1927. Like *No Hero for the Kaiser* by Rudolf Frank, which was published in Germany in 1931, it reflects a profound disillusionment with World War I.

Even now, there are relatively few novels for children about World War I. As Mary Cadogan and Patricia Craig (1978) note, aspects of that war are not easily isolated to create a theme; World War I tends to serve primarily as a general background for a story. They speculate that there might have been a reaction by authors and publishers against the blatantly propagandistic children's stories which were in print during the war. Cadogan and Craig also point out that in England, at least, World War I did not involve children as directly as World War II did. For most British (and American) children, life went on as usual. Schools were not evacuated, and contributions to the war effort were limited to such activities as knitting socks. It may have been difficult, therefore, for authors to create convincing child protagonists or plot lines involving children with such sketchy material to work with.

Three of the more interesting novels to emerge later about World War I involve young people's reactions to and/or relationships with adults who have been profoundly damaged by the war. In Cynthia Voigt's *Tree by Leaf* (1988), Clothilde's father's face and soul have both been scarred, and he has retreated from the world. The child is left alone to try to cope with his rejection, and only a mystical Voice can guide the child to reconciliation and understanding. In *After the Dancing Days* (1986), Margaret Rostkowski also presents a seriously wounded veteran as a symbol of the war's legacy. The young protagonist and her mother come to represent different, opposing social and personal responses to the consequences of war. Penelope Farmer's *Charlotte Sometimes* (1969) also includes a chilling scene in which the girl from contemporary times who has slipped in time back to World War I watches a train give up its grisly load of grotesquely wounded soldiers. The overall impression of World War I in children's literature available today is one of terrible human waste.

One important book from the period between the two world wars is *The Story of Ferdinand* by Munro Leaf (1936). While it does not allude to war in any way, its theme of nonviolence was probably interpreted as an anti-war or isolationist message at the time of its publication.

World War II presents a considerably more ambivalent face in children's literature. Two wartime novels for children which have survived on library shelves in my community are *Snow Treasure* by Marie McSwigan (1942) and *I Go by Sea, I Go by Land* by Pamela Travers, published originally in 1941. While *Snow Treasure* does present fairly stereotypical characterizations of bullying, stupid German soldiers and wily, heroic Norwegian resistance workers, it is a good adventure story in which children play an important role. *I Go by Sea, I Go by Land*, on the other hand, is flawed by the intrusion of the author's didactic voice and arch tone into what is meant to be a child's diary. It could only have been written in an effort to justify and win support for the British government's policy of relocating children from the cities. Its reprinting in the 1960s is more likely to have been due to the presumed marketability of its noted author than any literary merit of its own.

World War II affected authors who did not write about it directly. In Chapter 1, I discussed Esther Forbes' comparison of the Revolutionary War portrayed in *Johnny Tremain* (1943) with the war then being fought in Europe. *The Matchlock Gun* by Walter Edmonds (1941) is another Newbery winner which portrays a courageous defense against ferocious invaders. The defenders are Dutch settlers in upstate New York; the invaders are Indians; the context is the French and Indian War. The portrayal of the Indians as inhuman savages and the settlers as righteous defenders of their homes seems to anticipate the racist portrayal of the Japanese soldiers in American propaganda following the bombing of Pearl Harbor in 1941.

Sheila Egoff (1988) has written that World War II affected many writers of children's fantasy. Certainly the concept of heroic participation in a just war is central to the Narnia chronicles by C.S. Lewis. Egoff also sees the influence of World War II in the need to create peaceful, comforting images to counteract its horror. *Rabbit Hill* by Robert Lawson (1944) is a particularly poignant example, and E.B. White's *Charlotte's Web* (1952) may be its spiritual successor. It is not surprising that events as world-shattering as war should affect writers; it would be more surprising perhaps if they did not. In his study of children's books about the Revolutionary War, Joel Taxel (1984) found that the content tended to reflect the values and ideologies of the time in which the books were written, rather than an objective historical perspective.

In England, World War II was called "The People's War" (Cadogon and Craig 1978, p. 213). The civilian population, including children, was encouraged to participate actively in the war effort. Children collected scrap metal, volunteered with the Red Cross, tended victory gardens, and dreamed of fighting off any Nazi invasion of Great Britain. Many British children were removed from their homes to safer rural locations in an unprecedented evacuation policy that created a unique shared experience for a whole generation. British writers who were children during World War II look back on the period with a golden glow of nostalgia. Robert Westall's *The Machine Gunners* (1976) is about a group of children who are carried away by their intent to achieve glory by fighting off the German invasion forces. Michael Foreman's *War Boy* (1989) is a memoir that captures the childlike delight he must have felt when wearing a miniature uniform, collecting cigarette cards, or huddling in the Anderson shelter with his Mum. He makes the point at the end of his account that it all came right at the end.

> So it was true, all the things the grown ups had said during the dark days. Now the war was over everything would be all right, there'll be blue birds over the white cliffs, not barrage ballons. And men with rainbows on their chests would, like my kite, come home.
>
> And the memory of those who passed through our village on the way to war will remain for ever with the ghosts of us children in the fields and woods of long ago. (Foreman 1989, p. 91)

Nina Bawden's stories of childhood evacuation experiences are also washed with nostalgia. In *Henry* (1988), the mother and children inhabit a strangely idyllic world in their billet in rural Wales far from the stress of besieged London. Reality seems to be suspended temporarily for the members of this family who find in the simple rural setting an opportunity to see each other and the natural world in a different way. *Carrie's War* (1973) also has this quality of idyllic unreality, as if the children were enchanted rather than merely evacuated.

Anna Freud's research on children in England during the war supports some of the reactions and memories of these adult writers looking back on their childhood experiences. She found that school children adjusted to the constant bombing during the Blitz with relative ease, being more delighted by the action than frightened by the danger. Good Freudian that she was, she worried about the long-term effects on children who were not being appropriately civilized out of their aggressive tendencies at this stage. She found that if removal from the bombing involved separating children from their mothers, this was more traumatic, particularly for children under the age of six, although many school-age children treated this as an adventure as well (Freud and Burlingham 1973).

Not surprisingly, memoirs of World War II by Jewish writers living in Europe have a remarkably different content and tone. With the exception of Anne Frank's diary, these were written by survivors of one of the most devastating attempts to annihilate a targeted group of people that the world has known. Hamida Bosmajian (1989) writes about the difficulties facing the concentration camp survivor in finding an appropriate narrative voice, particularly when writing for children. The survivor has had to somehow make sense of the concentration camp experience itself and then to cope with the fact of survival, with all of its associated feelings of responsibility and guilt. The motivation for communicating the experience is often ambivalent at best, part therapeutic, part ideological, part aesthetic. Add to this the problem of adapting the story to a child's level of maturity, and the narrative problems become nearly insurmountable. Bosmajian cites Ruth Minsky Sender's *The Cage* (1986) as a particularly effective effort. This is one of the most explicit Holocaust memoirs, intended for young people who are old enough to understand the historical context and to integrate its horrific content with their own life experiences. Sender's solutions is to write in the present tense, the past being always present to the narrator.

> Sender's voice throughout the present tense narrative is that of the sensitive and intelligent teenager talking to a somewhat younger sister. She does not analyze herself or interpret her experience; she simply presents it, though the reader familiar with holocaust literature always senses the implied author's careful choice and omission of detail. This limits the narrative point of view, but also enables the narrator to swerve from the profound self-implications often found in survivor autobiographies. (Bosmajian, 1989; p. 315)

Hans Richter has borne much of the burden for portraying in novels for children the experience of World War II from the point of view of a German child. The narrative problems associated with this are also great. Bosmajian finds that the anonymous first-person narrator of Richter's *Friedrich* (1970) exemplifies the "unmastered past" of postwar Germany. The narrator presents himself and the behavior of himself and his family in an objective chronology of events that leads inexorably to the death of the young Jewish boy who had been the narrator's neighbor and friend in his early childhood. While he does not excuse himself, neither does he appear to understand his behavior or to deal with it on an emotional level.

> In *Friedrich* the everyman narrator testifies to words said and heard, to deeds done and observed but without interpretation and discovery of meaning for himself and the society he lives in; therefore, he cannot redeem himself. . . . The text of his narrative hints at choked grief, but there is no letting go and no liberation for this witness. (Bosmajian, 1989, p. 313)

Two novels deal with the legacy of guilt that has lived on for both ordinary Germans and for war criminals. M.E. Kerr's *Gentlehands* (1978), set in the contemporary United States portrays an adolescent boy who must deal with his own conflicted feelings of loyalty, repellance, and betrayal when his worldly grandfather is unmasked as a notorious Nazi war criminal, a concentration camp official who played Puccini as he tortured his victims. In *The Visit* by T. Degens (1982), a contemporary German girl learns the unpleasant truth about the role her Aunt Sylvia played during World War II. *The Ark* by Margot Benary-Isbert (1953), on the other hand, presents a German family struggling to get back to normality after the war, troubled by the shortage of food and shelter and by their father's delayed return, but apparently unscathed by war guilt or responsibility.

Stories about the American homefront during World War II are too varied to be characterized, but a word needs to be said about the experience of Japanese-Americans as it is represented in children's literature. As a motif, the treatment of Japanese-Americans appears briefly in several books set in the United States during World War II—Margaret Poynter's *A Time Too Swift* (1990), Ella Leffland's *Rumors of Peace* (1979), and Sollace Hotze's *Summer Endings* (1991). Only two novels deal with the Japanese-American experience as a major focus, however—the autobiographical *Journey to Topaz* by Yoshiko Uchida (1985) and the remarkable *The Eternal Spring of Mr. Ito* by Sheila Garrigue (1985), set in Vancouver. One would expect more writers to have found compelling stories to tell about this unprecedented and unsavory incident in American history, one which involved children so dramatically.

The Korean War merits barely a footnote in the children's literature canon. Pearl Buck's sentimental *Matthew, Mark, Luke, and John* (1966) is the only novel in the bibliography which depicts the Korean War.

For all the controversy at the time, the Vietnam War produced few novels for young people while it was being fought. The novels which were written later have tended to deal with the legacy of the war, rather than with the war itself. Thus, we have Katherine Paterson's *Park's Quest* (1988) and Candy Dawson Boyd's *Charlie Pippin* (1987), both dealing with children's efforts to discover what the war meant to their fathers, one dead and one living. In *December Stillness* by Mary Hahn (1988), an adolescent girl tries to learn more about a local homeless man who is a Vietnam veteran, and in the process, learns more about her own father as well. Diane Kidd's *Onion Tears* (1991), Maureen Wartski's *A Boat to Nowhere* (1980), and Khanh Tuyet Tran's *Little Weaver of Thai-Yen Village* (1987) are all about Vietnam War refugees.

The mid-1980s produced a spate of books about nuclear fear and the threat of nuclear war. *The Butter Battle Book* by Dr. Seuss (1984) and *Nobody Wants a Nuclear War* by Judith Vigna (1986) were intended for young children. Most of the nuclear fear books, however, were marketed as young adult titles. In *Nuclear Age Literature for Youth* (1990), Millicent Lenz discusses the implications of nuclear fear in adolescent literature. She sees a fundamental problem in defining heroism in a a nuclear age; the threat of nuclear destruction seems to make heroic action obsolete. Adolescents still need heroes to emulate, however, and a desirable future to anticipate. Many of the young adult novels with a nuclear theme explore the tension between those adolescent needs and the threat of destruction. Some, such as Lynn Hall's *If Winter Comes* (1986) and Stephanie Tolan's *Pride of the Peacock* (1986), are realistic novels in which contemporary young people confront their fears and come to terms with them. Some of the most interesting treatments, however, use the conventions of science fiction or fantasy to try to visualize life after a nuclear holocaust. Whitley

Streiber's *Wolf of Shadows* (1985) and Robert Swindells' *Brother in the Land* (1985) take place in the days and weeks immediately following a nuclear attack. *Children of the Dust* by Louise Lawrence (1985) presents a new society consisting of an entirely new and more developed species which has emerged to replace *homo sapiens* following a nuclear disaster. These novels enable young people to imagine themselves in otherwise unimaginable scenarios and ask themselves how they would respond to the challenges that are posed. They offer hope against a backdrop of despair.

It is probably too soon to evaluate the children's books that have been written about the Persian Gulf War. The nonfiction titles were rushed to publication to meet a perceived information need, and they reflect a consistently patriotic and noncritical point of view. Books like *"My Desert Storm" Workbook* (1991) had therapeutic purposes. Only the epistolary novel, *The War Began at Supper: Letters to Miss Loria* by Patricia Reilly Giff (1991), has a genuinely childlike approach and some literary merit beyond its didactic usefulness. It has been all too evident since the war in the Persian Gulf that there are very few children's books that present the Middle East with any objectivity; the Arab perspective is almost totally lacking.

I see two trends emerging in the 1990s in books for children and young people dealing with war and peace. One is a reconsideration of World War II, probably inspired by the fiftieth anniversary of American involvement in the war beginning in 1991. A welcome aspect of this trend is that some of these, such as Jane Yolen's *All Those Secrets of the World* (1991) are for very young children. The second trend is a new globalism and the inclusion of more non-Western voices in the canon of children's literature. Margaret and Raymond Chang's *In the Eye of War* (1990) and Sook Nyul Choi's *Year of Impossible Goodbyes* (1991) present Chinese and Korean perspectives on World War II, a welcome counterpoint to the many European and American chronicles. Children's Book Press continues to bring stories from third world countries to American children; some of these, such as Manlio Argueta's *The Magic Dogs of the Volcanoes* (1990) are concerned with the condition and effects of war. I suspect we will see more books like *My Grandmother's Journey* by John Cech (1991) which tell about refugees from war-torn countries. I hope that we will see the experiences of African-American and Latino people represented in the books that are forthcoming; their voices are sadly missing in this bibliography.

Major Themes and Issues

I will not attempt to catalog all the themes presented in the 400 children's books about war and peace that are included in this bibliography. However, some of the major recurring themes and issues should be noted.

Tension Between the Futility and the Nobility of War

Donnarae MacCann, like Anne Scott MacLeod, sees children's books as cultural artifacts, mirroring the prevailing ideas of the day. In an essay on militarism in juvenile fiction, she writes that many books about war are so filled with nostalgia that the real horrors of war are obscured. She finds a few exceptions to simplistic patriotism in books written after the 1950s, but overall the children's literature canon ". . . shows the persistence of militaristic codes, untempered nationalism and nostalgic visions of suffering and triumph" (MacCann 1982, p. 18). She urges that novels about war be written for children with assumptions ". . . that will disarm bigotry, militaristic biases and nostalgic delusions" (p. 20).

While MacCann criticizes what she sees as a militaristic bias in children's fiction, Carolyn Kingston finds that children's novels about war offer genuine tragic moments, ". . . a series of tragic essences that build toward a climax, which results in a new understanding of the problem" (Kingston 1974, p. 4). She finds that the context of war offers the opportunity for literary characters to find themselves or define themselves in a setting that is totally unlike everyday reality. The situation of war

> produces high stands of courage for some persons and a disintegration of all semblance of humanity in others. It also welds generally disassociated groups into a marvelous unity, a state of mind prolific of acts of self-sacrifice for the common cause. Emotional pitches of mystical ecstasy are reached. (Kingston 1974, p. 98)

While it is possible to cite titles from the bibliography which either promote militarism or provide an opportunity for heroic self-sacrifice, depending on your reading, my own interpretation of the body of children's literature about war is that much of it reflects both the futility and the nobility of war, often expressing a tension between the two. To make my case, I will briefly discuss several examples: a picture book for young children, two novels for middle-grade children, and two novels for young adults.

Once Upon a Dinkelsbuhl by Patricia Lee Gauch (1977) uses Tomie De Paola's irrepressible, childlike illustrations to retell a German medieval legend about a series of invasions by foreign armies that leave the people of Dinkelsbuhl hungry and in despair. As the Swedish army prepares yet another invasion, the townspeople are nearly too worn down to mount any kind of resistance; but they begin to make the usual preparations. The children of the town have another idea, however. They offer to share the last bits of food and clothing left in the village with the hungry, tattered Swedish soldiers. The soldiers are figuratively disarmed by the children's kindness and spare the town. This is a variation of the child as peacemaker theme that recurs in anti-war literature and propaganda, effectively combined with a message of nonviolent resistance. It is much more a story about how to make peace than it is a story about how to make war, although it is set in the context of a real war.

Avi's *The Fighting Ground* (1984) is a short novel with a fifth or sixth grade reading and interest level. A thirteen-year-old boy runs off to fight the Revolutionary War, armed with a borrowed musket and dreams of heroism. His small band of ill-equipped, untrained volunteers soon encounters a troop of Hessian soldiers. The Americans are quickly scattered and defeated by the Hessians, and Jonathan is captured. Now he sees first-hand what soldiers really do and the deaths that result. He succeeds in escaping but derives no heroic satisfaction from the deed, only relief at being alive. Disillusionment with the reality of warfare is a common experience for the young protagonists who actually experience combat first-hand.

In *Charley Skedaddle* by Patricia Beatty (1987), a twelve-year-old veteran of the mean streets of New York, thinks he's a tough kid when he joins the Union Army as a drummer boy. But he discovers that the chaos and fear of battle are more than he can handle, however, and he deserts. He ultimately finds self-respect not in warfare but in the wise counsel and sane life-style of an old mountain woman in Tennessee who gives him refuge.

In *The Machine Gunners* by Robert Westall (1976), the protagonists are British young people living in a seacoast village during World War II. Their village has been heavily bombed, and the children have taken to collecting shrapnel, competing over such prizes as nose cones or casings from exploded bombs. An opportunity to move beyond such child's play to the real business of war occurs when they find and salvage a real operating machine gun on a downed German warplane. They decide to set it up in a secret, strategic location and do their part when the Germans finally invade. It all ends badly, of course, with the young people mistaking a troop of Polish soldiers for the invading Germans and firing the gun with predictably disastrous results. Westall provides many ambiguities for the young reader to ponder. The young protagonists often seem as much at war with the adult authorities in their town as with the Germans. The tension between the promise of hope and glory which the children hope to achieve with their military valor and the disillusioning reality which actually results is not overplayed, but it gives complexity and subtlety to what otherwise might have been just another nostalgia piece.

In *My Brother Sam Is Dead* (1974), James and Christopher Collier present a view of war as not just futile but as totally absurd. The young protagonist watches his father and brother become estranged as they take opposite sides in the Revolutionary War. Their confrontation, and by implication, the war itself, becomes meaningless when both are killed in separate pointless incidents.

Heroism

Heroism offers much of the same ambiguity in children's novels about war. Some of the stories present their protagonists with opportunities for displays of courage and heroism that would not exist in peacetime. Thus we see young Lije Tully in Patricia Beatty's *Jayhawker* (1991) avenging his father's death at the hands of Southern marauders by spying on Quantrill's Confederate raiders. In Walter Edmonds' *The Matchlock Gun* (1941), ten-year-old Edward fires the old Spanish gun to protect his wounded mother, sister, and the family home from attacking Indians. Another ten-year-old, Annemarie Johansen, stands up to four German soldiers and delivers an important secret package to her uncle in Lois Lowry's *Number the Stars* (1989). In Michael Morpugo's *Waiting for Anya* (1991), a young boy risks his life to help protect the Jewish children who are trying to flee from Vichy France into Spain. Twelve-year-old Motele joins the Jewish partisans hiding in the forests of the Ukraine and plays an important role in bombing the Nazi headquarters in a nearby town in Yuri Suhl's *Uncle Mischa's Partisans* (1973). These are not everyday peacetime exploits.

In addition to the stories about wartime heroism, there are also stories about wartime disillusionment, about opportunities for heroism that have gone sour or lost their meaning in the carnage and waste. One of the more interesting presentations of this theme for young readers is *Rain of Fire* by Marian Bauer (1983). Young Steve has built up his big brother into a great war hero in order to impress his friends. When he comes home from his tour of duty in occupied Japan, Steve's brother has no exciting war stories to tell, so Steve makes them up, with unfortunate consequences. In *The Last Mission* by Harry Mazer (1979), the fifteen-year-old protagonist bluffs his way into the Army Air Corps and sees plenty of action flying bombing missions over Europe. It all seems exciting until his best buddy dies and he is captured by the Germans. He returns home a hero nonetheless, but he turns the conventions of the war adventure novel upside down by rejecting the glory and giving an anti-war speech at an assembly called to honor the military heroes of his high school.

Other novels present more unconventional definitions of heroism away from the frontlines. In Kathleen Kudlinski's *Hero Over Here* (1990), a little boy feels left out because there seem to be no opportunities for heroism on the home front. He gets his chance, however, when the Spanish flu strikes his town, and he must take care of his mother and sister. Georgie, the protagonist of Jane Langton's *The Fragile Flag* (1984), is actually an anti-war heroine, leading a march of thousands of children to protest the president's high tech weaponry. For the most part, however, the opportunities for heroic deeds of fortitude and valor are lacking in the quieter novels about peace and conflict resolution.

Survival

Not surprisingly, stories written for children about childhood war experiences tend to focus on survivors rather than victims. Some of the survival stories emerging from the situation of war are truly remarkable, focusing on a different kind of heroism than the conventional wartime model of courage, valor, and derring-do. In the wartime survival stories, the heroic qualities of courage and valor are extended by qualities of faith, hope, and persistence.

The survival stories themselves split into two categories. In the first type, the survivors are lone wolves who survive because of their own cunning. The protagonist in *Gideon* by Chester Aaron (1982) is a tough, cynical survivor of the Warsaw Ghetto and the Treblinka concentration camp. As a teenager in the Warsaw Ghetto, Gideon rejects his parents' moral position and collaborates with Polish thugs to operate a successful smuggling enterprise. Only when his father kills himself and a German soldier in order to save Gideon's life does he begin to think of anything other than his own well-being. His odyssey from that moment to participation in the Warsaw uprising to his work with a band of partisans to his confinement in and escape from Treblinka is still characterized by a kind of stubborn refusal to look closely at his own motivations as anything other than self-serving. It is almost as though he believes that altruistic behavior would jeopardize his efforts to survive.

A story with a very different setting but a similar disturbing message is Robert C. O'Brien's *Z for Zachariah* (1975). Here a sixteen-year-old girl has survived a nuclear attack and seems to be the only person left alive. When a man walks into her valley, she cares for him and rejoices in the possibility that the human race will survive. Ironically, she learns that she has more to fear from this fellow human being than from the radiation. Appropriately, both *Z for Zachariah* and *Gideon* are targeted for young adult readers, rather than for younger children. Young adults who are working to define their own identities in a world of other human beings are fascinated with just such paradoxes of human relationships.

In counterpoint to these lone survivors are the protagonists of Sook Nyul Choi's *Year of Impossible Goodbyes* (1991) and Yoko Kawashima Watkins' *So Far from the Bamboo Grove* (1986). In both of these stories, family members escape from perilous situations. Both authors make clear that it is family loyalty that holds the survivors together and gives them the strength to endure. In Uri Orlev's *The Island on Bird Street* (1984), an eleven-year-old boy hides out in an abandoned building in the Warsaw Ghetto. He is quite alone, but he is sustained by the hope that he will be reunited with his father. Both *The Silver Sword* by Ian Serraillier (1960) and *The Little Fishes* by Erik Christian Haugaard (1967) present bands of children on their own in the devastation of post-war Europe. Their survival depends on their ability to cooperate and support each other.

The survival theme is one of the most persistently appealing to child readers. Whether they crave the adventure because their own lives seem safe and boring or whether they feel empowered by the literary children who overcome dangers even greater than the ones that loom in their own lives, many children find these among the most satisfying of the realistic novels available to them. Highlighting survival themes is one way for adults to introduce historical novels to children who otherwise avoid anything but contemporary fare.

The Child Observer

A device that is used very effectively in many of the novels about war is the child observer. Presenting the story from a child's point of view enables the author to present just that part of the situation that a child would be able to see or to portray events without much adult explanation, leaving the interpretation up to the child reader as well as the child in the novel. Ida Vos does this effectively in *Hide and Seek* (1991), a novel about a childhood spent hiding from the Nazis in Holland. One senses the child's bewilderment and her feeling that events are spinning out of control. Young Sookan, the protagonist of *Year of Impossible Goodbyes* (1991), is puzzled by events that are occurring around her and by adult reactions to them. The author doesn't explain either, although there are clues in the text that the more sophisticated child or adult could understand.

Sometimes the child observer is looking back on past events, trying to make sense of family history. Charlie Pippin, in Candy Boyd's *Charlie Pippin* (1987), and Park, in Katherine Paterson's *Park's Quest* (1988), try to unravel the threads of their fathers' experiences in Vietnam. Jenny, in Doris Orgel's *A Certain Magic* (1976), reads Aunt Trudl's childhood diary and searches for the truth about her aunt's experiences as a refugee in England. In *The Devil's Arithmetic* (1988), Jane Yolen stretches this device by sending a child back in time to observe and participate in the events of the Holocaust.

A Critical Perspective

Virtually any approach to literary criticism that has been applied to literature for adults can be and has also been applied to literature for children, from structuralism to reader-response theory to semiotics. A good summary of these approaches can be found in Peter Hunt's *Criticism, Theory, and Children's Literature* (1991). The "Children's Literature" section of the bibliography includes some representative books and articles that use different critical approaches to treat the topics of war and peace in children's books. I would like to discuss just one critical problem and one literary theory in some detail, because I feel that they are particularly relevant to any thematic approach to children's literature, and particularly to a discussion of themes of war and peace in books for children and young people. The critical problem is ideology; the literary theory is reader-response theory.

The Issue of Ideology

Elsewhere in this book, I have talked about children's literature as cultural artifact, carrying the imprint of the values and customs of the society which produced it. This includes political values and ideologies, the beliefs and tenets of particular social segments or institutions. When the ideological message is overt, the text is seen as didactic, with an intent to teach a particular message or communicate a particular point of view. Didacticism almost always detracts in some way from the literary merit of a text or from the reader's aesthetic response. As Rebecca Lukens (1986, p. 118) points out: "If the information displaces the understanding, then didacticism has won out. Literature on the other hand, does not teach; it helps us understand." Didactic texts rarely achieve their objectives; children are likely to reject books that teach or preach while pretending to tell a story. This will not stop well-intentioned adults from writing or sharing such books with children, however. Moral tales have been around since at least the time of Aesop, and even such distinguished novelists as Umberto Eco occasionally succumb to the impulse to preach when they write for children.

Some children's books have been written as propaganda, with an express doctrinaire purpose. I have already cited P.L. Travers' *I Go by Sea, I Go by Land* as an example of wartime propaganda. Christa Kamanetsky (1984) has written a fascinating study of the children's literature that was produced as propaganda to socialize the new Aryan generation to the social and political ideology of Nazi Germany.

Children's books with an overt ideological message are frequently subject to censorship if the ideological message does not agree with the values of the adult who is intermediating between the book and the child. The censorship can be institutional, as when a librarian or teacher chooses not to include a particular book in a collection because the point of view is controversial or antithetical to the purpose of the sponsoring organization. Censorship can be a matter of national policy. In Nazi Germany, books which did not support regime values were burned. It is frequently more personal, as when a parent chooses not to read a particular story to a child because it is too violent. Censorship is not always caused by ideological content, of course; the parent may object to the violence because of the child's tender age, not because of an objection to the literary depiction of violence per se. Underlying most considerations of ideology in literature for children, however, are the notions that ideas are particularly powerful and are somehow legitimized when they appear in print and that children are particularly susceptible to the influence of ideas in print.

Peter Hollindale writes that the world of people who care about both children and books has split into two camps—the book people and the child people.

The result is a crude but damaging conjunction of attitudes on each side, not as it necessarily is, but as it is perceived by the other. A concern for the literary quality of children's books as works of imagination has become linked in a caricatured manifesto with indifference to the child reader and with tolerance or approval of obsolete, or traditional or "reactionary" political values. A concern with the child reader has become linked with indifference to high standards of literary achievement and with populist ardour on behalf of the three political missions which are seen as most urgent in contemporary society: anti-racism, anti-sexism, and anti-classism. (Hollindale 1988, p. 5)

Using Hollindale's classification scheme, we can assign critics like Donnarae MacCann, whose objection to militarism in children's books has been noted earlier, to the "child" camp. Almost any of the writers who talk about "using" books with children, myself included, tend to stray into this category. Aligning herself on the other side, with the "book" people, is Natalie Babbitt, who argues against the point of view that literature should be purposeful: "If a book isn't first of all a pleasure, then it can't do any good no matter how literary it may be or how useful to present needs, because nobody will read it" (Babbitt 1990, pp. 151-52).

As Hollindale sees it, the dichotomy between book people and child people is ironic and tragic because it prevents us from looking beyond the surface trappings of a text to the layers where the most powerful ideological messages are carried, transmitted through the author's own values and beliefs to the very fabric of the story. The Marxist critic Terry Eagleton (1983, p. 194) points out that it isn't necessary to drag politics into literature or literary theory; it has always been there. Thus, while Natalie Babbitt's own *The Search for Delicious* (1969) is by no means a didactic or political novel, it is imbued with an anti-war message that informs the character development, the plot structure, even the language itself. It is also a pleasure to read.

Hollindale notes that the child/book dichotomy also has the effect of focusing our attention on what children read, rather than how they read. And this leads to a brief discussion of reader-response theory.

Reader-Response Theory

The reader-response, or audience-centered, approach to criticism focuses its attention on the relationship between the reader and the text, rather than on the text alone or on the relationship between the author and the text. Within this broad definition, there are a number of distinct subcategories which need not concern us here. A good introduction to the range of thinking within this approach is *The Reader in the Text*, edited by Susan Suleiman and Inge Crosman (1980). What is significant about this approach to literary criticism for people who care about both children's literature and about children is that it allows us to think about the child's response to a text as a unique experience with a number of variables, most particularly, the child's past experiences with books and with life. It allows for the different frames of reference—literary, developmental, situational, and cultural—that each reader brings to his or her understanding of a literary work. It allows us to think about the meaning of a text in the context of multiple readers, who assign their own meanings based on their own frames of reference, and encourages us to think about building communities of shared meaning. Susan Steinfurst reminds us that the reader-response method allows children to be introspective and to be taken seriously, ". . .as active readers and interpreters as we and no better or worse." (Steinfurst 1986, p. 115).

This is a particularly important insight to keep in mind as you delve into the bibliography that follows this chapter and into the books that are listed there. War and peace are critical topics for human beings to understand. Literature can help us develop that understanding. Written from the heart, as well as the mind, with the skill and creativity and insight that the best authors for children bring to the task, literature can help us see our world differently. That may not be its purpose, as Natalie Babbitt so eloquently declared, but it is a consequence of the best novels. We will all respond differently, but we will all gain something from the experience. For children who have experienced war first-hand, good books may help them to understand and then cope with the horrors they have lived through. For children who have experienced war only through the medium of television, well-written stories may give a human dimension to their framework for understanding. For all children, literature may offer both the motivation and the tools to work for peace. Literature can be the bridge between readers of all backgrounds, offering new visions and new possibilities, new frameworks for understanding each other and the world. And yes, literature can also be a pleasure.

At bottom, I disagree with Natalie Babbitt, although I love her books. A meaningful literary encounter is not always a pleasure. It is painful to read Toshi Maruki's *Hiroshima No Pika* (1980). Whitley Streiber's *Wolf of Shadows* (1985) is a disturbing novel and Hans Richter's *Friedrich* (1970) is upsetting. *Conrad's War* by Andrew Davies (1980) is provocative, not pleasant. While individual reader responses may vary, it is safe to say that most people will find reading these books to be unpleasant. Few readers would be untouched, however, by their encounters with them. Literature that touches us leaves us forever changed by the experience. There are many books on the pages that follow that will touch you and the children in your world and leave you forever changed.

References

Babbitt, Natalie. (1990). "The Purpose of Literature: Who Cares?" *School Library Journal*, Vol. 36, No. 3, 150-52.

Bosmajian, Hamida. (1989). "Narrative Voice in Young Readers' Fictions About Nazism, the Holocaust, and Nuclear War." In Charlotte F. Otten and Gary D. Schmidt, editors. *The Voice of the Narrator in Children's Literature*. New York: Greenwood, 308-24.

Cadogan, Mary, and Patricia Craig. (1978). *Women and Children First: The Fiction of Two World Wars*. London: Victor Gollanca.

Eagleton, Terry. (1983). *Literary Theory: An Introduction*. Minneapolis: University of Minnesota Press.

Egoff, Sheila A. (1988). *Worlds Within: Children's Fantasy from the Middle Ages to Today*. Chicago: American Library Association.

Freud, Anna, and Dorothy T. Burlingham. (1973). *War and Children*. Westport, CT: Greenwood Press.

Hollindale, Peter. (1988). "Ideology and the Childen's Book." *Signal*, No. 55, 3-22.

Hunt, Peter. (1991). *Criticism, Theory, and Children's Literature*. Oxford, UK/Cambridge, MA: Blackwell.

Kamanetsky, Christa. (1984). *Children's Literature in Hitler's Germany: The Cultural Policy of National Socialism*. Athens, OH: Ohio University Press.

Kingston, Carolyn T. (1974). *The Tragic Mode in Children's Literature*. New York: Teachers College Press.

Lenz, Millicent. (1990). *Nuclear Age Literature for Youth: The Quest for a Life-Affirming Ethic*. Chicago: American Library Association.

Lukens, Rebecca J. (1986). *A Critical Handbook of Children's Literature*, third edition. Glenview, IL: Scott, Foresman.

MacCann, Donnarae. (1982). "Militarism in Juvenile Fiction." *Interracial Books for Children Bulletin*, Vol. 13, Nos. 6 & 7, 18-20.

MacLeod, Anne Scott. (1985). "An End to Innocence: The Transformation of Childhood in Twentieth-Century Children's Literature." In Joseph H. Smith and William Kerrigan, editors. *Opening Texts: Psychoanalysis and the Culture of the Child*. Baltimore: Johns Hopkins University Press, 100-17.

Steinfurst, Susan. (1986). "Reader-Response Criticism." *School Library Journal*, Vol. 32, No. 2, 114-15.

Suleiman, Susan R., and Inge Crosman, editors. (1980). *The Reader in the Text: Essays on Audience and Interpretation*. Princeton, NJ: Princeton University Press.

Taxel, Joel. (1984). "The American Revolution in Children's Fiction: An Analysis of Historical Meaning and Narrative Structure." *Curriculum Inquiry*, Vol. 14, No. 1, 7-55.

Children's Books Cited

Aaron, Chester. (1982). *Gideon*. New York: Lippincott.

Alcott, Louisa May. (1968). *Little Women*. Boston: Little, Brown.

Argueta, Manlio. (1990). *The Magic Dogs of the Volcanoes*. San Francisco: Children's Book Press.

Avi. (1984). *The Fighting Ground*. New York: Lippincott.

Babbitt, Natalie. (1969). *The Search for Delicious*. New York; Farrar, Straus and Giroux.

Bauer, Marion Dane. (1983). *Rain of Fire*. New York: Clarion.

Bawden, Nina. (1973). *Carrie's War*. New York: Harper & Row.

———. (1988). *Henry*. New York: Morrow.

Beatty, Patricia. (1988). *Be Ever Hopeful, Hannalee*. New York: Morrow.

———. (1987). *Charley Skedaddle*. New York: Morrow.

———. (1991). *Jayhawker*. New York: Morrow.

———. (1984). *Turn Homeward, Hannalee*. New York; Morrow.

Benary-Isbert, Margot. (1953). *The Ark*. New York: Harcourt.

Boyd, Candy Dawson. (1987). *Charlie Pippin*. New York: Macmillan.

Buck, Pearl. (1966). *Matthew, Mark, Luke, and John*. New York: John Day.

Cech, John. (1991). *My Grandmother's Story*. New York: Bradbury.

Chang, Margaret, and Raymond Chang. (1990). *In the Eye of War*. New York: McElderry/Macmillan.

Choi, Sook Nyul. (1991). *Year of Impossible Goodbyes*. Boston: Houghton Mifflin.

Collier, James Lincoln, and Christopher Collier. (1974). *My Brother Sam Is Dead*. New York: Four Winds.

Davies, Andrew. (1980). *Conrad's War*. New York: Crown.

Degens, T. (1982). *The Visit*. New York: Viking.

Edmonds, Walter D. (1941). *The Matchlock Gun*. New York: Dodd, Mead.

Farmer, Penelope. (1969). *Charlotte Sometimes*. New York: Harcourt Brace Jovanovich.

Forbes, Esther. (1943). *Johnny Tremain*. Boston: Houghton Mifflin.

Foreman, Michael. (1989). *War Boy*. New York: Arcade.

Frank, Rudolf. (1986). *No Hero for the Kaiser*. New York; Lothrop, Lee, & Shepard.

Garrigue, Sheila. (1985). *The Eternal Spring of Mr. Ito*. New York: Bradbury.

Gauch, Patricia Lee. (1977). *Once Upon a Dinkelsbuhl*. New York: Putnam.

Giff, Patricia Reilly. (1991). *The War Began at Supper: Letters to Miss Loria*. New York: Dell.

Hahn, Mary. (1988). *December Stillness*. New York: Clarion.

Hall, Lynn. (1986). *If Winter Comes*. New York: Scribner.

Haugaard, Erik Christian. (1967). *The Little Fishes*. Boston: Houghton Mifflin.

Hotze, Sollace. (1991). *Summer Endings*. New York: Clarion.

Kerr, M.E. (1978). *Gentlehands*. New York: Harper.

Kidd, Diane. (1991). *Onion Tears*. New York: Orchard.

Kudlinski, Kathleen V. (1990). *Hero Over Here*. New York: Viking.

Langton, Jane. (1984). *The Fragile Flag*. New York: Harper.

Lawrence, Louise. (1985). *Children of the Dust*. New York: Harper & Row.

Lawson, Robert. (1944). *Rabbit Hill*. New York: Viking.

Leaf, Munro. (1936). *The Story of Ferdinand*. New York: Viking.

Leffland, Ella. (1979) *Rumors of Peace*. New York: Harper.

Lowry, Lois. (1989). *Number the Stars*. Boston: Houghton Mifflin.

Maruki, Toshi. (1980). *Hiroshima No Pika*. New York: Lothrop.

Mazer, Harry. (1979). *The Last Mission*. New York: Delacorte.

McSwigan, Marie. (1942). *Snow Treasure*. New York: Dutton.

Morpugo, Michael. (1991). *Waiting for Anya*. New York: Viking.

Mukerji, Dhan Gopal. (1927). *Gay-Neck: The Story of a Pigeon*. New York: Dutton.

Murphy, Jim. (1990). *The Boys' War: Confederate and Union Soldiers Talk About the Civil War*. New York: Clarion.

"My Desert Storm" Workbook: First Aid for Feelings. (1991). New York: Workman.

O'Brien, Robert C. (1975). *Z for Zachariah*. New York: Atheneum.

Orgel, Doris. (1976). *A Certain Magic*. New York: Dial.

Orlev, Uri. (1984). *The Island on Bird Street*. Boston: Houghton Mifflin.

Paterson, Katherine. (1988). *Park's Quest*. New York: Dutton.

Poynter, Margaret. (1990). *A Time Too Swift*. New York: Atheneum.

Reeder, Carolyn. (1989). *Shades of Gray*. New York: Macmillan.

Richter, Hans. (1970). *Friedrich*. New York: Holt.

Rostkowski, Margaret. (1986). *After the Dancing Days*. New York: Harper & Row.

Sender, Minsky. (1986). *The Cage*. New York: Macmillan.

Serraillier, Ian. (1960). *The Silver Sword*. New York: Criterion.

Seuss, Dr. (1984). *The Butter Battle Book*. New York: Random.

Streiber, Whitley. (1985). *Wolf of Shadows*. New York: Knopf.

Suhl, Yuri. (1973). *Uncle Mischa's Partisans*. New York: Four Winds.

Swindells, Robert. (1985). *Brother in the Land*. New York: Holiday House.

Tolan, Stephanie. (1986). *Pride of the Peacock*. New York: Scribner.

Tran, Khan Tuyet. (1987). *Little Weaver of Thai-Yen Village*. San Francisco: Children's Book Press.

Travers, P.L. (1964). *I Go by Sea, I Go by Land*. New York: Norton.

Uchida, Yoshiko. (1985). *Journey to Topaz: A Story of the Japanese-American Evacuation*. Berkeley, CA: Creative Arts.

Vigna, Judith. (1986). *Nobody Wants a Nuclear War*. Niles, IL: Whitman.

Voigt, Cynthia. (1988). *Tree by Leaf*. New York: Atheneum.

Vos, Ida. (1991). *Hide and Seek*. Boston: Houghton Mifflin.

Wartski, Maureen. (1980). *A Boat to Nowhere*. Louisville, KY: Westminster.

Watkins, Yoko Kawashima. (1986). *So Far from the Bamboo Grove*. New York: Lothrop.

Westall, Robert. (1976). *The Machine Gunners*. New York: Greenwillow.

White, E.B. (1952). *Charlotte's Web*. New York: Harper & Row.

Yolen, Jane. (1991). *All Those Secrets of the World*. Boston: Little, Brown.

———. (1988). *The Devil's Arithmetic*. New York: Viking.

Resources

Remembering Other Wars: Real and Imaginary

Stories for Young Children

Ambrus, Victor G. *Brave Soldier Janosch.* New York: Harcourt, Brace, & World, 1967.
> An old Hungarian soldier tells tall tales about his extraordinary feats of courage in battle to a crowd of spellbound villagers and one skeptical student. (Grades Kindergarten-2)

Argueta, Manlio. *Magic Dogs of the Volcanoes/Los Perros Magicos de los Volcanes.* Translated from the Spanish by Stacey Ross. Illustrated by Elly Simmons. San Francisco: Children's Book Press, 1990.
> A bilingual story by a noted Salvadoran author. When the government sends lead soldiers to attack the legendary magic dogs who protect the people living in the mountains, the volcanoes erupt in anger. When the soldiers start to melt, they realize that they must give up their military pursuits and take up more worthy professions. (Grades Kindergarten-3)

Baker, Betty. *The Pig War.* Illustrated by Robert Lopshire. New York: Harper & Row, 1969.
> American farmers and British soldiers each think the island they are on belongs to them. Eventually a war starts when some British pigs wander off into an American garden. Fortunately, the conflict is soon resolved, and the British sail away, leaving the island in American hands. This "I Can Read History Book" would be improved by a historical note giving the name of the island and the date of the incident. As it stands, however, it is a simple account of how easily wars can begin—and end. (Grades 2-3)

Benchley, Nathaniel. *George the Drummer Boy.* Illustrated by Don Bolognese. New York: Harper & Row, 1977.
> The opening events of the American Revolution at Lexington and Concord are presented from the point of view of a British drummer boy. (Grades 2-3)

————. *Sam the Minuteman*. Illustrated by Arnold Lobel. New York: Harper & Row, 1969.

A very easy text tells about a boy who participates in the Battle of Lexington at the beginning of the Revolutionary War. (Grades 2-3)

Bunting, Eve. *How Many Days to America? A Thanksgiving Story*. Illustrated by Beth Peck. New York: Clarion, 1988.

A family from an unnamed Latin American country flees their village when the soldiers come. A harrowing boat ride eventually takes them to the United States, where people welcome them on the shore. Not all refugees are welcomed so warmly, of course, but this is an optimistic story about new beginnings. (Grades Kindergarten-3)

————. *The Wall*. Illustrated by Ronald Himmler. New York: Clarion, 1990.

A small boy and his father find the name of the boy's grandfather on the Vietnam Veterans Memorial in Washington. The details and tone are just right for young children. (Grades Kindergarten-3)

Cech, John. *My Grandmother's Journey*. Illustrated by Sharon McGinley-Nally. New York: Bradbury, 1991.

Korie's grandmother tells her the stories Korie likes best, stories about her own life, beginning when she was a little girl in Russia. She grows up, marries, and lives through the turmoil and hardships of the Russian Revolution. She has a baby (who will grow up to be Korie's mother) and survives the Nazi invasion and a German labor camp before coming to the United States. It is a story shared by many immigrants to this country, and a story well told. (Grades Kindergarten-3)

Clifton, Lucille. *Amifika*. Illustrated by Thomas DiGrazia. New York: Dutton, 1977.

Amifika's Daddy has been away in the army so long that the little boy hardly remembers him. Now Daddy's army days are over and he's coming home, but Amifika worries that there won't be room for both his Daddy and him in their small apartment. There is a splendid reunion, however, when Amifika ". . . jumped in the man's arms and squeezed his arms around the man's neck just like his arms remembered something." (Grades Preschool-Kindergarten)

Gauch, Patricia Lee. *Once Upon a Dinkelsbuhl*. Illustrated by Tomi De Paola. New York: Putnam, 1977.

In this retelling of a medieval German legend, the children of Dinkelsbuhl take matters into their own hands when the town is invaded by a foreign army for the fourth time. Instead of fighting back, however, the children offer the hungry, tattered Swedish soldiers bread and clothing. The soldiers are figuratively disarmed by the children's kindness and spare the town. (Grades Kindergarten-3)

————. *This Time, Tempe Wick?* Illustrated by Margot Tomes. New York: Coward McCann & Geogehegan, 1974.

In many respects, this easy-reading fictional account is a more successful portrayal of the legendary Revolutionary War heroine than the full-length novel for older readers by Ann Rinaldi. Tempe Wick is seen here as a spirited, raw-boned farm girl who came up with a clever way to hide her favorite horse from the mutineering Revolutionary soldiers. (Grades 2-4)

Hest, Amy. *Love You, Soldier.* New York: Four Winds, 1991.

Seven-year-old Katie's father goes off to fight World War II. She misses him, and she knows that her mother does too because she hears her crying at night. As time goes by, other people fill up some of the empty space left by the soldier father. Her mother's pregnant friend comes to stay with them, and soon there is baby Rosie as well. An elderly neighbor joins them often for meals and companionship. Yet when word comes that her father has been killed, Katie has to deal with that permanent loss and learn to take risks in loving all over again. A childlike, perceptive, little novel. (Grades 2-4)

Houston, Gloria. *The Year of the Perfect Christmas Tree.* Illustrated by Barbara Cooney. New York: Dial, 1988.

It is the turn of Ruthie's family to provide their Appalachian town with its Christmas tree. Before her father leaves to fight World War I in Europe, he shows Ruthie the perfect balsam he has picked to be their gift. Armistice is declared before Christmas, and other soldiers begin to return, but not Ruthie's father. She and her mother cut the tree themselves, and the village Christmas program goes on. When the presents are passed out, there is a special present for Ruthie and her mother—Papa has come home. (Grades Kindergarten-3)

Lobel, Anita. *Potatoes, Potatoes.* New York: Harper & Row, 1967.

This anti-war fable tells the story of a war between the East and the West, fought for no apparent reason and resulting in much suffering and hardship. Hunger and concern for their mothers make the soldiers stop fighting. Although its resolution of the conflict is simplistic, the book successfully portrays the horror of battle, primarily through its illustrations. (Grades Kindergarten-3)

Lyon, George Ella. *Cecil's Story.* Illustrated by Peter Catalanotto. New York: Orchard, 1991.

Haunting paintings and a minimal text tell of a young boy's thoughts and fears when first his father goes off to fight the Civil War and then his mother leaves to find his father. While the setting is historical, the child's feelings are timeless. (Grades Kindergarten-3)

Mattingley, Christobel. *The Angel with a Mouth-Organ.* Illustrated by Astra Lacis. New York: Holiday House, 1984.

A mother tells her two children the story of the glass angel that traditionally tops their Christmas tree. It is a story of the plight of civilian refugees in a war-torn land, of deaths and separations, an ultimate reunion with a lost father, and a new beginning in a new land. The pictures show the setting to be Europe during

World War II, but the story is that of many refugees from many wars in many lands. (Grades 2-4)

Pene du Bois, William. *The Forbidden Forest*. New York: Harper & Row, 1978.

In his characteristic farcical style, the author/illustrator creates an imaginary end to World War I. In his version, the Germans are sabotaged by a boxing kangaroo, her human boxing partner, and a bulldog. The dedication to Jane Fonda and the tongue-in-cheek approach to militarism suggest an anti-war message, but it is obscured by the violent tactics used by the three unlikely heroes to end the war. (Grades 2-4)

Ray, Deborah Kogan. *My Daddy Was a Soldier: A World War II Story*. New York: Holiday House, 1990.

A little girl shares her experiences, thoughts, and feelings she had during the time when her daddy was a soldier in World War II. Details about victory gardens, scrap metal drives, and ration books bring the period alive. Young readers will understand both Jeannie's fears for her father's safety and her loneliness. (Grades 2-4)

Say, Allen. *The Bicycle Man*. Oakland, CA: Parnassus Press, 1982.

The author recreates a childhood memory of a Sportsday in his Japanese village just a year after the end of World War II. Two American soldiers show up, the first the children had ever seen. At first the children are frightened, but the Americans seem friendly. The black soldier asks to ride the principal's bicycle and dazzles the crowd with his trick riding. They respond by giving him first prize, and he thanks them in Japanese. A believable story of *rapprochement* between two former enemies. (Grades 2-4)

Schackburg, Richard. *Yankee Doodle*. Illustrated by Ed Emberley. New York: Prentice-Hall, 1965.

Barbara Emberley's notes provide background about the Revolutionary War as well as the song. The woodcuts are stunning to look at and authentic in their historical detail. This is a treat to share with young children. (Grades Preschool-2)

Schick, Alice, and Marjorie N. Allen. *The Remarkable Ride of Israel Bissell . . . As Related by Molly the Crow*. Illustrated by Joel Schick. Philadelphia: Lippincott, 1976.

This simple picture book tells the story of the post rider who carried the news of the start of the American Revolution from Boston to Philadelphia. (Grades Kindergarten-2)

Seuss, Dr. *The Butter Battle Book*. New York: Random, 1984.

This is Dr. Seuss's metaphorical depiction of the nuclear arms race. Young children tend to respond to the book on more concrete and personal levels, however. See "*The Butter Battle Book*: Uses and Abuses with Young Children" by Nancy Carlsson-Page and Diane E. Levin (listed in "Parenting, Teaching, Guiding" section of this bibliography) for a discussion of appropriate uses of this book with young children. (Grades Kindergarten-3)

Tran, Khanh Tuyet. *The Little Weaver of Thai-Yen Village/ Co be tho-det lang Thai-yen*. Translated from the Vietnamese by Christopher N.H. Jenkins and Tran-Khanh-Tuyet. Illustrated by Nancy Hom. San Francisco: Children's Book Press, 1987.

> In this bilingual story, war comes to Hien's village in Vietnam, killing her family and seriously wounding her. She is sent to the United States for a special operation. Hien worries that she will never return to her own people again and finds comfort in the blanket that she weaves and sends back to Vietnam. (Grades 2-4)

Wild, Margaret. *Let the Celebrations Begin!* Illustrated by Julie Vivas. New York: Orchard, 1991.

> While the brief text and large illustrations suggest that very young children are the intended readers for this picture book, it would probably be best to use it with children who are at least eight years old. An older child who can still remember a happy life at home tells the younger children in the concentration camp about toys and other small joys of everyday, normal life. Then she and the women in the camp begin to make toys for the small children, toys that will be used to celebrate their imminent liberation by the Allied soldiers. While there is charm and poignancy in this story which chronicles the triumph of the human spirit in inhuman circumstances and while it is based on a true incident, there is some danger that it will misrepresent the facts of the Holocaust. The facts are that few young children survived in the death camps; they were killed upon arrival. Even at the "model camp" of Terezin, designed as a transit camp and show case for visiting foreigners, only 100 children survived out of the 15,000 who passed through. The children that the women at Belsen made toys for may have been children that they hoped to meet on the outside. It is unlikely that there were any living children in Belsen when it was liberated by the British. (Grades 2-4)

Yolen, Jane. *All Those Secrets of the World*. Illustrated by Leslie Baker. Boston: Little, Brown, 1991.

> In this nostalgic picture book, four-year-old Jane's father leaves to be a soldier in World War II. The little girl learns some of the secrets of the world, the ones about big and little, near and far, war and peace. (Grades Preschool-2)

Zeifert, Harriet. *A New Coat for Anna*. Illustrated by Anita Lobel. New York: Knopf, 1986.

> Set in an unnamed European country just after World War II, this is the simple story of a series of trades and exchanges that results in a new coat for a little girl. The war is only suggested in illustrations of bombing damage in the city. Adults may have to explain to young children why there were no coats, hardly any food, and little money when the war was over. (Grades Kindergarten-3)

Novels for Children

Aaron, Chester. *Alex, Who Won His War*. New York: Walker, 1991.
Loosely based on an actual incident, this novel tells the story of two young boys in Pequod, Connecticut, who get entangled with two German spies when they find a dead body washed up on the shore. Alex and his friend Larry face a moral dilemma as they decide whether to endanger the lives of two local women being held hostage by telling the authorities about the Nazis who have infiltrated the town. (Grades 6-8)

Alcott, Louisa May. *Little Women*. Illustrated by Jessie Willcox Smith. Boston: Little, Brown, 1968.
In the introduction to this centennial edition, Cornelia Meigs reminds us that Alcott served as a volunteer nurse in a Washington hospital during the Civil War. Her best-known novel, published in 1868, deals not with the battle front, however, but with the women left at home. The story opens with the four little women talking about the cheerless Christmas they will be having, with their father off at the war, and no presents because Marmee said they should not be spending money for pleasure when the soldiers were suffering. The war remains a part of the fabric of their lives for the rest of the first part of the novel. (Grades 6-8)

Alphin, Elaine. *The Ghost Cadet*. New York: Holt, 1991.
When twelve-year-old Benjy meets the ghost of a military school cadet who was killed in the Civil War battle of New Market, he has the opportunity to give the cadet's missing watch to his heirs and restore the cadet's good name. In the process, Benjy acquires a new sense of self-worth. (Grades 5-7)

Anderson, Margaret J. *Searching for Shona*. New York: Knopf, 1978.
Two dissatisfied orphan girls living in Edinburgh—one with her wealthy Uncle Fergus and the other at St. Anne's Orphanage—impulsively change identities at the train station as they are being taken from the city during World War II. Uncle Fergus' "niece" goes off to Canada, and we don't hear much more about her. The new orphanage girl, now known as Shona, is sent to the country where she and another orphan, Anna, live with two elderly twin spinsters. There are air raids and food shortages and clothing coupons, but the war is less important to the story than the themes of family and identity. The war ends, and both girls choose to remain who they have come to be rather than reclaim their real identities. (Grades 6-8)

Arnold, Elliott. *A Kind of Secret Weapon*. New York: Scribner's, 1969.
The secret weapon is the underground paper that Peter's parents publish and distribute as part of the Danish resistance to the Nazi occupation government. Peter's political education is escalated when his father is arrested and killed, leaving him and his mother vulnerable but determined to carry on the work. (Grades 5-8)

Avi. *The Fighting Ground*. New York: Lippincott, 1984.
Thirteen-year-old Jonathan goes off to fight in the Revolutionary War with a borrowed musket and dreams of heroism. Reality comes soon enough, when the

small band of volunteers encounters a troop of Hessian soldiers. Jonathan is captured and sees first-hand the real work that soldiers do and the death that results. He returns home without his dreams but happy to be alive. (Grades 6-8)

Babbitt, Natalie. *The Search for Delicious*. New York: Farrar Straus and Giroux, 1969.

In this fantasy, a kingdom comes to war over competing definitions of the word "delicious," but only after the evil Hemlock has stirred up the dissent and cut off the water supply. The writing is felicitous, and the anti-war message unobtrusive. (Grades 5-7)

Baillie, Allan. *Little Brother*. Australia: Nelson, 1986.

Vithy makes his way alone across Cambodia to the Thai border, evading the Khmer Rouge, eating off the land, and hoping to meet with his older brother Mang as they had agreed. The happy ending is somewhat contrived and unrealistic, but this is in other ways a compelling novel about a child's struggle to survive as a refugee from one of the most grotesque civil wars in our memory. (Grades 6-8)

Baker, Betty. *The Dunderhead War*. New York: Harper & Row, 1967.

In 1846, Quince and his Uncle Fritz from Germany journey from Independence, Missouri, to Santa Fe on a trading mission, only to find themselves in the middle of the Mexican War. The historical background is integral to the plot but adds surprisingly little to the reader's understanding of the Mexican War. (Grades 6-8)

Bauer, Marion Dane. *Rain of Fire*. New York: Clarion, 1983.

When Steve's big brother comes home after his experiences as a soldier in occupied Japan, he has no exciting war stories to tell, so Steve makes them up. The consequences are disastrous, but the twelve-year-old ultimately learns important truths about himself and about the complexities of war. (Grades 5-7)

Bawden, Nina. *Carrie's War*. New York: Harper & Row, 1973; Dell, 1989.

Twelve-year-old Carrie and her younger brother Nick are evacuated from London to a small town in Wales. They live with a harsh, stingy shopkeeper and his dominated sister, and existence is bleak until they make friends with the assorted members of a nearby household. World War II is even more remote in this haunting novel than it is in the author's other story about young British evacuees, *Henry*. One senses that for Bawden, World War II was a time of suspended reality in which children experienced themselves and their new surroundings in unexpected and unusual ways. (Grades 5-8)

————. *Henry*. New York: Morrow, 1988; Dell, 1990.

A young girl tells about the baby squirrel who comes into her family's life at the same time the family begins experiencing life as evacuees in rural South Wales. "Tipped out of his old life, as we had been tipped out of ours when the bombing got bad and we had to leave London, he was at home in his new life from the beginning, as at home in our sitting room as we were at home on the farm." (pp. 9-10). The father is far away, on a convoy ship sailing between England and the United States; the war seems remote as well, a shadowy background of blackout curtains; infrequent, static-filled news bulletins; and the occasional letter from Dad. Henry, the lively squirrel, provides the mother and children with a more immediate distraction. The narrator provides a nostalgic look back at World War II, a time when this family found themselves in a simpler, strangely peaceful setting. War must seem like this to many young people, especially those who are self-absorbed with the onset of adolescence, for whom the agony of having to be seen entering an outdoor lavatory is more critical than the knowledge that bombs are falling 200 miles away. (Grades 6-8)

Beatty, Patricia. *Charley Skedaddle*. New York: Morrow, 1987.

Charley Quinn is only twelve years old, but he's one of the Bowery Boys and proud of his fighting skills. He joins the Union Army as a drummer boy, only to discover that fighting on the battlefield is much different than fighting on the streets of New York. He deserts and finds refuge and new self-respect with an old mountain woman in Tennessee. This is a well-researched historical novel, with memorable characters and a unique perspective on the Civil War. (Grades 5-7)

———. *Jayhawker*. New York: Morrow, 1991.

Beatty brings to life another small episode of the Civil War in this story about a young Jayhawker, a Kansas abolitionist, who serves as a spy for the Union Army by joining up with the bushwhacking Confederates who serve with Quantrill. (Grades 6-8)

———. *Turn Homeward, Hannalee*. New York: Morrow, 1984.

When the invading Yankees discover that the mill in Roswell, Georgia, has been making cloth for the Confederate Army, the mill is shut down and the workers are sent up north to work—including twelve-year-old Hannalee and her little brother, Jem. Disguised as a boy, Hannalee escapes from the Kentucky family where she has been assigned, finds her brother, and makes her way back home. *Be Ever Hopeful, Hannalee* (Morrow, 1988) continues the story of Hannalee and her family as they and the South try to rebuild after the war. Beatty has tried to tell the story of poor Southern whites during the Civil War and presents a perspective often lacking in books for young people. (Grades 6-8)

Beatty, Patricia, and Phillip Robbins. *Eben Tyne, Powdermonkey*. New York: Morrow, 1990.

This novel about a Virginia boy who serves as a powdermonkey on the ironclad *Merrimack* is stronger on naval strategy and operations than it is on plot or character development, but it does chronicle an important Civil War event that is otherwise relatively untouched in children's literature. (Grades 5-8)

Benary-Isbert, Margot. *The Ark*. Translated from the German by Clara and Richard Winston. New York: Harcourt, 1953.

A leisurely, idealized account of an ordinary German family trying to put its life back in order after World War II. The father is still missing, presumably in a Russian prison camp; a brother has been killed; the family home has been destroyed and the mother and remaining children relocated. There is little acknowledgment of German culpability for the horrors of World War II here;

the subtext appears to be that there were decent Germans who should not be blamed for the horrors committed by the government. However, these adults may seem too quietly heroic and the children too well-behaved to be completely credible. (Grades 6-8)

Bencastro, Mario. "A Clown's Story." In Lori M. Carlson and Cynthia L. Ventura, editors, *Where Angels Glide at Dawn: New Stories from Latin America*. Illustrated by Jose Ortega. New York: Lippincott, 1990.

A clown talks about how difficult it is to make people laugh when their country is in the middle of a civil war. The author is a Salvadoran writer and painter now living in the United States. (Grades 6+)

Bergman, Tamar. *Along the Tracks*. Translated from the Hebrew by Michael Swirsky. Boston: Houghton Mifflin, 1991.

This is the odyssey of Yankele, separated from his mother and little sister while they are fleeing from the German army. He wanders along the railroad tracks through much of the southern part of the Soviet Union for four years until he is miraculously reunited with his mother who has been working the entire time on a collective farm near one of his frequent stops. The family is even more miraculously reunited with the father who had been assumed dead. In spite of the unlikely plot, the young hero is plucky and appealing and a believable survivor. (Grades 6-9)

———. *The Boy from Over There*. Translated from the Hebrew by Hillel Halkin. Boston: Houghton Mifflin, 1988.

Jewish children in the kibbutzim of the Jordan Valley had sacrificed during World War II, but their experiences were mild compared with the children who survived the Holocaust "over there" in Europe. This is the story of a boy from over there and his slow adjustment to life on a kibbutz. When Israel's independence is declared by the United Nations and the Arabs of the region in return wage war on the new nation, Avramik proves to be a leader among the children. The point of view is clearly Israeli; readers will have to search elsewhere for the Arab point of view. (Grades 4-6)

Berleth, Richard. *Samuel's Choice*. Illustrated by James Watling. Niles, IL: Whitman, 1990.

Samuel is the slave of a wealthy farmer in Brooklyn during the Revolutionary War. The choice that he makes in this short novella is to assist the rebels and win his own independence. (Grades 3-5)

Bishop, Claire Huchet. *Pancakes-Paris*. Illustrated by Georges Schreiber. New York: Viking, 1947.

In postwar France, food is still severely rationed. While Charles can remember the prewar tradition of eating crepes for Mardi Gras, it seems impossible that they will do so this year—until two American soldiers contribute their box of pancake mix. (Grades 3-5)

————. *Twenty and Ten*. Illustrated by William Pene Du Bois. New York: Macmillan, 1952.

> This is a short novel about 20 French Catholic children who are sent away to the mountains for safety during World War II. They agree to shelter 10 Jewish children who are in hiding from the Nazis. They learn that this means both sacrifice—they must share their scarce rations with the refugees—and danger, when the Germans come looking for the children. The story's religious context and pious, self-congratulatory tone may be off-putting to some, but it is still worthwhile as an account of children's heroism during wartime. (Grades 4-6)

Blume, Judy. *Starring Sally J. Freedman as Herself*. Scarsdale, NY: Bradbury, 1977.

> World War II has been over for two years, but Sally is convinced that Hitler is still alive and living in her apartment building in Florida! (Grades 4-6)

Boyd, Candy Dawson. *Charlie Pippin*. New York: Macmillan, 1987; Puffin, 1988.

> Eleven-year-old Charlie senses that her demanding father had been changed in some way by his experiences as a soldier in Vietnam, but he won't talk about it. Her efforts to understand what the Vietnam War meant to him and to other black soldiers lead finally to a forbidden trip to Washington to see the Vietnam Memorial and an emotional reconciliation with her father. (Grades 5-7)

Buck, Pearl S. *Matthew, Mark, Luke, and John*. Illustrated by Mamoru Funai. New York: John Day, 1966.

> The unrealistic happy ending and sentimental tone detract from the value of this story about four boys who have been abandoned by their American fathers and Korean mothers in the aftermath of the Korean war. (Grades 3-5)

Bunting, Eve. *Terrible Things*. Illustrated by Stephen Gammell. New York: Harper & Row, 1980.

> Adult readers will interpret this animal fable as an allegory about the Holocaust. Children who don't see that reference will be able to comprehend the message about the importance of standing together against evil and oppression. This book could generate much discussion. (Grades 4+)

Burchard, Peter. *Jed: The Story of a Yankee Soldier and a Southern Boy*. New York: Coward-McCann, 1960.

> While doing picket duty at his Union Army camp deep in Mississippi, sixteen-year-old Jed encounters a young Southern boy who has broken his leg. He asks the army surgeon to set the boy's leg and then returns him to the small farm where he lives with his mother and sister. There, Jed experiences human warmth and friendship that transcend the ideologies and geography of the Civil War. (Grades 5-8)

Caudill, Rebecca. *Tree of Freedom*. Illustrated by Dorothy Bayley Morse. New York: Viking, 1949; Puffin, 1988.

> The story of a pioneer family starting out in Kentucky in 1780 is presented from the point of view of thirteen-year-old Steffie. Differing points of view about the Revolution being fought to the East are represented by the individualistic father

who resists all forms of government as unwarranted invasions on his liberty and the idealistic son who joins Colonel Marion to fight for the liberty that he feels will be ensured by independence from Great Britain. (Grades 5-8)

Chaikin, Miriam. *Aviva's Piano*. Illustrated by Yossi Abolafia. New York: Clarion, 1986.

A rocket attack from across the Lebanese border has the unexpected consequence of creating a big enough hole in the wall of Aviva's house that her new piano can be moved in. This easy-reading story set in a a kibbutz in the north of Israel reflects the conventional Israeli perspective, referring to the bombing of the kibbutz simply as a terrorist attack. Some adults may want to provide children with more background about the conflict between Israel and her Arab neighbors. (Grades 3-5)

Chang, Margaret, and Raymond Chang. *In the Eye of War*. New York: McElderry/Macmillan, 1990.

Japanese-occupied Shanghai is seen through the eyes of ten-year-old Shao-Shao. As part of a middle-class Chinese family, he is removed from most of the consequences of the war. The effects of the war on Shao-Shao are almost more poignant for their everyday quality—his crush on a neighbor girl whose father is shunned as a collaborator, the ever-present Japanese soldiers, the hated Japanese lessons in school, his father's clandestine resistance work. The portrayal of the Japanese surrender as it was experienced by the people of Shanghai is vivid. For another story about a childhood experience of the war in China, see Meindert DeJong's *The House of Sixty Fathers*. (Grades 5-7)

Choi, Sook Nyul. *Year of Impossible Goodbyes*. Boston: Houghton Mifflin, 1991.

This autobiographical novel about life in Korea during the turbulent years of Japanese and Russian occupation during and immediately after World War II is full of the small details of domestic life in a time of hardship. Seen from the perspective of a ten-year-old girl, some of the military and political events are only half-understood. Adults will understand, for example, why the young Korean women are so horrified at the prospect of being sent to be "spirit girls" for the Japanese soldiers, while child readers will be as puzzled as young Sookan was. The children's solitary escape from North Korea is heroic. (Grades 4-6)

Climo, Shirley. *A Month of Seven Days*. New York: Crowell, 1987.

A feisty Georgia girl tricks the superstitious Yankee captain who has requisitioned her family's home into thinking that it's haunted. (Grades 5-7)

Coerr, Eleanor. *Sadako and the Thousand Paper Cranes*. Illustrated by Ronald Himler. New York: Putnam, 1977.

The moving story of a Japanese girl who died of leukemia as a result of exposure to the atomic bomb that destroyed Hiroshima. Her courage, hope, and lack of bitterness made her a heroine to the children of Japan as well as a symbol of the universal desire for peace. (Grades 3-5)

Cohen, Barbara. *The Secret Grove*. Illustrated by Michael J. Deraney. New York: Union of American Hebrew Congregations, 1985.

> A young Israeli man remembers a childhood encounter with an Arab boy that transcended the prejudices and stereotypes each had been taught by adults. (Grades 3-5)

Collier, James Lincoln, and Christopher Collier. *War Comes to Willy Freeman*. New York: Delacorte, 1983; Dell, 1987.

> Thirteen-year-old Willy Freeman sees her father killed by a British bayonet and then learns that her mother has been taken prisoner. Disguised as a boy, she first makes her way to her uncle Jack Arabus but leaves quickly when it appears that his master will try to sell her back into slavery. At the end of the war, her mother is released, only to die for lack of medical care for the fever she has caught while working on a British prison ship. Willy sees that independence for the colonies will not bring freedom to blacks or better conditions for women. The plot is convoluted and the characters are flat, but the historical details are sound in this first volume of the Arabus family saga which continues with *Jump Ship to Freedom* and *Who Is Carrie?* This is also one of the few novels which portrays black Americans during the Revolutionary War. (Grades 6-8)

Cormier, Robert. *Other Bells for Us to Ring*. Illustrated by Deborah Kogan Ray. New York: Delacorte, 1990.

> Eleven-year-old Darcy Webster finds her first best friend when her wandering family lands in Frenchtown. Kathleen Mary O'Hara seems to be everything Darcy is not—Irish, Catholic, red-headed, and bold. Darcy's father goes away to World War II, and Kathleen Mary just goes away. When they receive word that Sergeant Webster is missing in action, Mrs. Webster turns inward and Darcy turns to the Catholic nun who Kathleen Mary claimed could work miracles. World War II is the backdrop for this story, but the deaths take place at home, not on the battleground. Darcy witnesses a suicide and learns at last of Kathleen Mary's tragic death. Introspective readers will gather much from this deeply felt and finely wrought novel about love and faith and the fragility of human life. (Grades 6-8)

Davies, Andrew. *Conrad's War*. New York: Crown, 1980.

> Conrad likes wars, armies, killing, guns, and his dog Towzer. He is not very surprised, then, when his daydreams of being a British soldier in World War II become remarkably real. The wit is wicked, and the time warp device is clever in this sophisticated novel about war play gone berserk. (Grades 6-8)

Degens, T. *Transport 7-41-R*. New York: Viking, 1974.

> After World War II, a thirteen-year-old German girl joins a transport train returning evacuees to Cologne from the Russian sector. The war has taught her to be ruthlessly independent and selfish in order to survive, but this journey teaches her the redeeming qualities of love and caring. (Grades 6-8)

————. *The Visit*. New York: Viking, 1982.

> A contemporary German girl discovers the unsavory truth about the role her Aunt Sylvia played during World War II as well as the fate of her long-dead Aunt Kate. (Grades 6-8)

DeJong, Meindert. *The House of Sixty Fathers*. Illustrated by Maurice Sendak. New York: Harper & Row, 1956.

> Here is a survival story set in Japanese-occupied China. Young Tien Pao is separated from his family when their sampan breaks loose and is carried far into Japanese territory. Young Tien Pao not only survives a harrowing trek through rough, enemy-occupied territory, but he saves his pet pig and an American airman as well. The 60 fathers are members of an American bomb squadron who look after the lost boy and help him find his parents. The rural setting and the child's encounters with real soldiers and real bullets make this an interesting contrast with Margaret and Raymond Chang's *In the Eye of War*, which is set in Shanghai. An added bonus in DeJong's story is the poignant black-and-white art by Maurice Sendak, done in the early years of his career as an illustrator. (Grades 4-6)

Edmonds, Walter D. *The Matchlock Gun*. Illustrated by Paul Lantz. New York: Dodd, Mead, 1941.

> Based on a true incident, this is a novella about a Dutch family living in the Hudson River Valley in 1756, during the French and Indian War. While the father is away with the militia, a band of Indians attacks the family's remote home. The mother is seriously injured by a tomahawk, but ten-year-old Edward succeeds in firing the old Spanish matchlock gun, killing three Indians and scaring off the rest. The book is marred by its stereotypical portrayal in both text and illustrations of Indians as inhuman savages. This is the description of the Indians as they approach the house: "They hardly looked like men, the way they moved. They were trotting, stooped over, first one and then another coming up, like dogs sifting up to the scent of food" (p. 39). It is not surprising, perhaps, that this book was awarded the Newbery Medal in 1941 as the most distinguished children's book published in the United States. That was a year when it must have seemed appropriate to reward heroic behavior while under attack by inhuman savages. (Grades 4-6)

Farmer, Penelope. *Charlotte Sometimes*. Illustrated by Chris Connor. New York: Harcourt Brace & World, 1969.

> Charlotte, a contemporary British child, finds herself switching places with Clare, a boarder at the same school in 1914. World War I is an ever present and significant background element in this time travel fantasy. In a chilling scene, wounded men disembark from a hospital train in a kind of "grotesque circus," and Charlotte wonders how the men had dared to go off to war, knowing they might end up like this. (Grades 4-6)

Fenton, Edward. *The Refugee Summer*. New York: Delacorte, 1982.

> In the summer of 1922, Greece is at war with Turkish Anatolia, but it seems remote to Nikolas, the son of the caretaker of an elegant villa in the suburbs of Athens, until the American family arrives. Together with the children visiting

at the neighboring villa, they form a gang to wage war against injustice and suffering caused by grown-ups. It is all child's play at first. Then the Turks burn the city of Smyrna, and the refugees arrive. A poignant story of class differences as well as a child's view of the consequences of war. (Grades 4-6)

Fleischman, Paul. *The Borning Room*. New York: HarperCollins, 1991.
On an Ohio farm, a daughter is born, grows up, marries, and has children of her own. Elsewhere, soldiers are fighting the battles of the Civil War. On a luminous day in April 1863, the girl shares with her grandfather the joy she has felt running free and seeing the wonders of the natural world. "Hundreds dead at Vicksburg," he said. "But a thousand births in those woods every minute. They shall all be reborn" (p. 41). This is an extraordinary, life-affirming novel that focuses on the small events in the history of a family, contrasting with the larger pageantry of history. (Grades 6+)

Garrigue, Sheila. *All the Children Were Sent Away*. New York: Bradbury, 1976.
Eight-year-old Sara is one of the thousands of children sent from her family in England to Canada to wait out World War II in a safer place. This is the story of her journey across the Atlantic on a great ocean liner in the company of Lady Drume. In spite of her guardian's disapproval, she makes friends with two Cockney children; they explore the ship and almost forget the war. It is only when the ship is torpedoed by a German U-boat and Ernie helps Lady Drume escape her smoke-filled cabin that the war becomes real again and Lady Drume abandons some of her class prejudices. Sara's reactions to the war and her evacuation are realistically childlike—she doesn't understand why the Germans are bombing her town; she doesn't want to die; she misses her family; she tries to be brave; and she finds in her play with the other children a happy escape from her worries and fears. (Grades 4-6)

―――. *The Eternal Spring of Mr. Ito*. New York: Bradbury, 1985.
In this independent sequel to *All the Children Were Sent Away*, Sara and Ernie are living in Vancouver with their Aunt and Uncle when Japan attacks Pearl Harbor. Sara has grown close to Mr. Ito, the family's gardener, who has given her a bonsai to raise. Now she sees the Ito family sent off to internment camps and Mr. Ito choose death rather than live with that dishonor. A disturbing book for thoughtful young readers. (Grades 6-9)

Gauch, Patricia Lee. *Thunder at Gettysburg*. Illustrated by Stephen Gammell. New York: Coward, McCann & Geoghegan, 1976.
A brief text, based on an actual eyewitness account, and evocative black-and-white drawings present the battle of Gettysburg as experienced by a fourteen-year-old resident of the town. (Grades 4-6)

Giff, Patricia Reilly. *The War Began at Supper: Letters to Miss Loria*. Illustrated by Betsy Lewin. New York: Dell, 1991.
This fictional account of the effect of the Persian Gulf War on American children is told entirely through the letters that one elementary school class writes to a beloved former student teacher. While the didactic purpose of this book is

evident, it succeeds in its sincerity and attentiveness to the concerns that children had during the war. It serves the needs of the children rather than a particular ideology. (Grades 3-5)

Glassman, Judy. *The Morning Glory War*. New York: Dutton, 1990.

Jeannie does her part for the war effort, collecting newspapers, starting a victory garden, and sending V-mail to a soldier pen pal, who seems to think that she is an adorable teenager rather than a chubby fifth grader. It isn't surprising that she sees her feud with Suzanne, her upstairs neighbor and the most popular girl in her class, as a kind of war as well. A realistic school story, with telling details about life in Brooklyn during World War II. (Grades 4-6)

Green, Connie Jordan. *The War at Home*. New York: McElderry/Macmillan, 1989.

Mattie's family moves from their home in the Kentucky mountains to Oak Ridge, Tennessee, where her father has found a job that he is not free to discuss. When the atomic bomb is dropped on Hiroshima, the true nature of his work is revealed. The author grew up in Oak Ridge, and this seems to be her effort to justify the work that was done there. She explains in an endnote that the celebration in Oak Ridge when the bomb was dropped and the war was over, which she describes in the book, " . . . sprang from the hope that there would be no more killing, not from a callous disregard for the death and destruction caused by the atomic bomb." Little insight about why the people at Oak Ridge felt as they did is provided by the novel itself, however. (Grades 5-7)

Hahn, Mary Downing. *Stepping on the Cracks*. New York: Clarion, 1991.

Margaret's brother Jimmy is fighting the Germans in Europe, but a bigger enemy on the home front is Gordy, the bully of the sixth grade. Margaret and her best friend discover Gordy's secrets—that his father beats him brutally and that he is hiding his brother Stuart, who deserted from the Army before being sent overseas. In spite of initial misgivings about giving aid and comfort to a deserter, the girls get involved in helping Stuart survive a bout of pneumonia. Maggie comes to respect Stuart's pacifist views, even after she receives news that Jimmy has been killed. In addition to its perspective on small-town life during World War II, the novel provides insights about family dynamics and adolescent self-discovery. (Grades 5-7)

Hartman, Evert. *War without Friends*. Translated from the Dutch by Patricia Crampton. New York: Crown, 1982.

Arnold has no friends because his father is a member of the Dutch National Socialist Party, a supporter of the Nazi regime occupying Holland. Arnold is ostracized, bullied, and severely beaten by classmates and ultimately renounces his father's politics. Unfortunately, neither his father's fanaticism nor Arnold's slow conversion are well-motivated; most young readers will be confused rather than enlightened. (Grades 6-8)

Haugaard, Erik Christian. *The Boy and the Samurai.* Boston: Houghton Mifflin, 1991.

Saru's mother died giving birth to him and his father was killed in the battle of Mikata-ga-hara. Raised for a time by a foster mother, he is orphaned a second time when he is six years old. Saru survives on his own in feudal Japan, during a period of civil wars that cause upheaval for everyone. (Grades 6-8)

——. *The Little Fishes.* Illustrated by Milton Johnson. Boston: Houghton Mifflin, 1967.

A first-person narrative about a boy left orphaned and homeless in Italy at the end of World War II. The tone is dark and introspective; much of the novel consists of Guido's own thoughts about the devastated lives he observes. (Grades 5-8)

Ho, Minfong. *The Clay Marble.* New York: Farrar Straus Giroux, 1991.

Twelve-year-old Dara and the remnants of her family flee from their village in Cambodia to a refugee camp on the Thai border. At first, the camp is safe and begins to feel like a community. Dara makes a friend, Jantu, who shows her how to make dolls and marbles out of clay and helps her find the self-confidence she needs to survive when the war comes to the refugee camp and Dara's world is torn apart once again. An eloquent survival story. (Grades 5-8)

Holman, Felice. *The Wild Children.* New York: Scribner, 1983.

A story about the *bezprizorni*, the "wild children" left orphaned and homeless in the turmoil following the Russian Revolution. Well researched, the novel is more memorable for its unusual subject matter than for elements of plot or characterization. (Grades 5-7)

Hoover, H.M. *Children of Morrow.* New York: Four Winds, 1973.

Tia and Rabbit are children living in a patriarchal, anti-technological society centuries after a nuclear disaster, "The Great Destruction," was followed by an ecological catastrophe, "The Death of the Seas." Their telepathic abilities, not shared by other people in their community, put them in touch with another group of survivors who have built a society based on unity and harmony between technology and nature. While Tia and Rabbit's desperate escape from their home after Rabbit kills one of the "Fathers" is an exciting survival story, the underlying themes are poorly developed and the writing is pedestrian. (Grades 5-7)

Hotze, Sollace. *Summer Endings.* New York: Clarion, 1991.

In this novel we see how World War II affected the lives of a variety of people in the United States. A twelve-year-old Polish-American girl's life changes over the last summer of the war. Christine and her mother have had no news about her father, a political prisoner in Poland. Her sister Rosie dances with sailors at the Aragon Ballroom, eventually marrying one of them and moving away. The hot dog vendor is proud of his son on a battleship in the Pacific. The Chens have been taken for Japanese so many times that they have added a big "Chinese" over their laundry sign. A skillful evocation of a working-class neighborhood in Chicago in 1945. (Grades 6-8)

Hunt, Irene. *Across Five Aprils*. Chicago: Follett, 1964.

> The four long years of the Civil War are seen through the eyes of a boy who is 10 years old and living in southern Illinois when Fort Sumter is fired on. One brother joins the Confederate Army; another brother dies fighting with the Union Army at Pittsburg Landing. His sister's fiancée is severely wounded. When a cousin deserts from the Union Army, Jethro writes to President Lincoln asking for advice, and the president writes back, promising amnesty for deserters who reenlist. It's a microcosm of the war from the perspective of a family living close to the border between North and South. (Grades 5-8)

Innocenti, Roberto, and Christophe Gallaz. *Rose Blanche*. Illustrated by Roberto Innocenti. New York: Stewart, Tabori & Chang, 1990.

> This is a welcome reissue of a stunning pictorial allegory of the Holocaust. A young German girl, whose name is an allusion to the White Rose, a German Resistance organization, watches the comings and goings of soldiers, tanks, and military trucks in her small town. One day she sees a little boy jump out of a truck and try to run away. She is curious and follows the truck out of town and deep into a forest. There she sees children standing behind electric barbed wire. They tell her they are hungry, and she gives them bread. For weeks, she secretly returns to the concentration camp, bringing food to the starving children. Then there is a sudden evacuation from her town as the Russian army moves in. Rose Blanche returns to the forest to find the concentration camp emptied. Soldiers are moving in the forest. There is a shot, and Rose Blanche is presumably killed, because she never returns to her mother. A highly emotional and effective introduction to the Holocaust and to the concept of social responsibility. The actual facts will have to come from other sources. (Grades 4+)

Jacques, Brian. *Mattimeo*. Illustrated by Gary Chalk. New York: Philomel, 1990.

———. *Mossflower*. Illustrated by Gary Chalk. New York: Philomel, 1988.

———. *Redwall*. Illustrated by Gary Chalk. New York: Philomel, 1986.

> These three books comprise the Redwall trilogy, about a community of animals living in an ancient abbey. These are intricate, swashbuckling adventure stories, full of the military exploits of small animals who try to emulate their hero, the great mouse, Martin the Warrior. There are also evil villains, like Cluny the Scourge, a savage rat. The wars fought within these pages are as complete with tactics, strategy, blood and gore as any fought on the pages of real history books. (Grades 6-8)

Jones, Cordelia. *Nobody's Garden*. Illustrated by Victor Ambrus. New York: Scribner, 1966.

> Thick-skinned, extroverted Hilary learns to be more sensitive when she befriends a shy, withdrawn girl whose parents both died during World War II. What could be a somewhat clinical case study of post traumatic stress syndrome is transformed into a convincing story in which friendship and the human spirit are triumphant. (Grades 5-7)

Kerr, Judith. *When Hitler Stole Pink Rabbit*. New York: Dell, 1987.
This is the story of one Jewish family's escape from Nazi Germany in 1933. For nine-year-old Anna, the experience is sometimes an adventure, but more often a confusing hardship. Contemporary readers will appreciate the details about adjusting to life as a refugee in a new country, and adults will see the underlying theme of family unity in this autobiographical novel. (Grades 4-6)

Kidd, Diana. *Onion Tears*. Illustrated by Lucy Montgomery. New York: Orchard, 1991.
Nam-Huong tells her own story about the cruelty of other children and the kindness of a few adults in her new Australian home. Letters to a remembered canary and duck in Vietnam reveal the horrors of the war that separated her from her family, perhaps forever. This is a moving portrait of a child traumatized by war. (Grades 4-6)

Kudlinski, Kathleen V. *Hero Over Here*. Illustrated by Bert Dodson. New York: Viking, 1990.
Theodore feels left out when first his father and then his older brother go off to fight World War I and be heroes "over there." Then the Spanish flu strikes his town, and both his mother and sister are ill. He manages to take care of them and to save the life of a man who has fallen ill among the hoboes by the railroad tracks. The author makes the point that opportunities for heroism are not limited to the battlefield. (Grades 3-5)

———. *Pearl Harbor Is Burning! A Story of World War II*. Illustrated by Ronald Himler. New York: Viking, 1991.
It is 1941, and Frank's family has just moved to Hawaii. As a newcomer and a *haole*, he feels miserable until he makes friends with Kenji, a Japanese-American boy. He shows Kenji his tree house and from that perch high above Pearl Harbor, the two boys witness the Japanese bombing of the U.S. naval fleet. This is a very short novella, and some issues remain unresolved at the end, including the anti-Japanese prejudice of Frank's mother. (Grades 3-5)

Lawson, John. *The Spring Rider*. New York: Crowell, 1968; Harper Trophy, 1990.
One hundred years ago, Jacob and Gray's great-great-grandfather fought on the Confederate side of a Civil War battle that took place near their Shenandoah Valley farm. Ghosts of soldiers appear every year to wage that battle over again; and the Spring Rider, Abraham Lincoln himself, appears to try to stop the fighting. The brother and sister from modern times become involved with the men from the past in this haunting fantasy. (Grades 6-8)

Lawson, Robert. *Mr. Revere and I*. Boston: Little, Brown, 1953.
The events leading up to the American Revolution, including Paul Revere's famous midnight ride, are told from the point of view of his horse, Scheherazade. This is irreverent history. (Grades 5-7)

Levitan, Sonia. *Journey to America*. New York: Macmillan, 1970.
The impending Holocaust is seen through the eyes of a young Jewish girl as first her father and then the rest of her family flee from Germany in 1938. The

emphasis in this autobiographical novel is on the uncertainties and hardships of the refugee experience for this one middle-class family. It is similar in tone and content to *When Hitler Stole Pink Rabbit* by Judith Kerr. *Silver Days* is the sequel, in which the immigrant family begins to make a life in the United States while the war takes its toll on family and friends left behind in Europe. (Grades 5-7)

Levoy, Myron. *Alan and Naomi*. New York: Harper & Row, 1977.

It is 1944 in New York, and Alan Silverman just wants to play stickball with his buddies. He reluctantly agrees to be friendly to Naomi upstairs, a refugee who has been traumatized by her war experiences in Nazi-occupied France. Slowly he wins her trust, and she wins his heart. There is no happy ending, however. When Naomi sees Alan attacked by a neighborhood bully, she retreats into a still more severe mental illness and must be hospitalized. A moving story about friendship and the effects of war on children. (Grades 6-8)

Lewis, C.S. "The Chronicles of Narnia."

Book 1. *The Lion, the Witch, and the Wardrobe*. Illustrated by Pauline Baynes. New York: Macmillan, 1950.

Book 2. *Prince Caspian*. Illustrated by Pauline Baynes. New York: Macmillan, 1951.

Book 3. *The Voyage of the "Dawn Treader."* Illustrated by Pauline Baynes. New York: Macmillan, 1952.

Book 4. *The Silver Chair*. Illustrated by Pauline Baynes. New York: Macmillan, 1953.

Book 5. *The Horse and His Boy*. Illustrated by Pauline Baynes. New York: Macmillan, 1954.

Book 6. *The Magician's Nephew*. Illustrated by Pauline Baynes. New York: Macmillan, 1955.

Book 7. *The Last Battle*. Illustrated by Pauline Baynes. New York: Macmillan, 1956.

Much has been written about the Christian theology and symbolism that pervades this much-loved series of fantasies set in the alternative world of Narnia. The underlying theme is usually described as the battle between good and evil. The operative word is battle, for these are among the most militaristic of children's novels. The first book opens with the four children being evacuated from the London Blitz to the strange old mansion where they find the wardrobe (or the country of War Drobe, as the animals in Narnia refer to it) that opens into the magical land of Narnia. Among the first enchanted happenings in that land is the gift of weapons from Father Christmas. With their weapons, the human children fight the first of the great battles that frees Narnia from the spell of the White Witch.

The battle becomes part of the heroic lore of Narnia, so that in Book 2, Prince Caspian will yearn for the ". . .wonderful old days when there were battles and adventures" (p. 39). Lewis means for us to understand that heroes fight when called on. In *The Voyage of the Dawn Treader*, Eustace is initially presented as a most unpleasant character and a pacifist; only when he learns to fight his battles bravely is he presented sympathetically. Bree is the Talking Horse featured in

The Horse and His Boy. Once a great war horse, he has been captured by the Calormene and put to more lowly uses. He reminisces: "Give me the Narnian war where I shall fight as a free Horse among my own people! Those will be wars worth talking about" (p. 23). Finally, in *The Last Battle*, the earthly world that the heroes have known comes to an end in a battle against the forces of evil. Eustace, now a great hero of Narnia, expresses the heroic ideal: "I'd rather be killed fighting for Narnia than grow old and stupid at home and perhaps go about in a bathchair and then die in the end" (p. 96).

Children who love these stories may be oblivious to the implied imperialism and racism (the human enemies in Narnia, the Calormene, are "darkies" from the south), but they can hardly avoid getting the message that it is heroic to fight and die for one's country. (Grades 5-7)

Lingard, Joan. *Tug of War*. New York: Lodestar/Dutton, 1990.
A Latvian family flees from the advancing Russian army in 1944. While the writing is undistinguished, this novel gives young readers a point of view that is unique in stories about World War II. Here Germany is presented as a place of refuge, while the Russians, an American ally, are shown as the historic enemy of the Latvian people. In addition to giving a fictional account of the experience of displaced persons after World War II, the writer provides insights into the contemporary political unrest in the Baltic states. In the sequel, *Between Two Worlds* (Lodestar/Dutton, 1991), the family adjusts to a new life in Canada. (Grades 6-9)

Little, Jean. *Listen for the Singing*. New York: HarperCollins, 1977; 1991.
World War II is presented here from the point of view of a severely vision-impaired girl who is a German immigrant in Canada. Anna is already struggling to adjust to a mainstream high school after attending special classes. The onset of World War II brings additional problems: anti-German sentiments, her family's concerns about relatives left behind in Germany, and her brother Rudi's decision to enlist. This may sound like a heavy burden of problems for one novel to bear, but Little succeeds in balancing it all and presenting Anna as a fully realized character. (Grades 5-8)

Lively, Penelope. *Going Back*. New York: Dutton, 1975.
This short, sophisticated novel is as much about memory as it is about World War II in an English country home. Among the characters that people this miniature world are land girls, a conscientious objector who changes his mind and joins the army, evacuees from London, a remote father, a caring housekeeper, and the two children whose story this is. (Grades 5-8)

Lowry, Lois. *Autumn Street*. Boston: Houghton Mifflin, 1980.
The first and last chapter frame this story as a memoir of an important year in a child's life. Elizabeth is only six in the remembered year, living with her mother, sister, and baby brother with her grandparents because her father has gone off to war. The war is significant as one of those imponderable aspects of adult life that is never really explained to Elizabeth. She becomes friends with Charles, the black cook's grandchild. The two children help each other try to

understand and cope with the perplexing world around them. But Charles is killed in a dreadful, violent incident, and Elizabeth's father loses a leg in the war. The older narrator who is remembering it all muses: "Probably my father and I both knew, even then, that it was not true, what we told each other, that bad things would never happen again. But we needed that lie, that pretending, the spring that I was seven. We had both lost so much. He had told me his secret: that sometimes, in the night, he felt a deep, unassuageable pain in the place where his leg had been; and I had whispered to him of mine, of the hollow place inside me where I ached with memory and with fear" (pp. 187-88). The author has captured perfectly the feelings of confusion, fear, and guilt that are part of the darker side of childhood. (Grades 5-7)

―――――. *Number the Stars*. Boston: Houghton Mifflin, 1989.
When she hears that the Germans who are occupying Denmark plan to take away all the Jews, ten-year-old Annemarie says that all the Danes must be bodyguards to the Jews; and soon enough she has a chance to play that role herself. The episode in which Annemarie faces four German soldiers as she delivers an important secret package to her uncle at his boat is taut with suspense. This is a quiet well-written story of honor and courage, a Newbery medal winner. (Grades 4-6)

Lunn, Janet. *The Root Cellar*. New York: Scribner, 1983.
Rose Larkin "shifts" from contemporary time to the world of the 1860s. She and Susan, a girl from the 1860s, go searching for Will who left his Canadian farm to join the Union Army and never returned home. Their difficult journey comes to an end in Washington, D.C., where they find Will, much saddened and aged by his experiences as a soldier. While this is primarily the story of how Rose learns to adjust to life in her own time and place, it also presents a realistic and devastating picture of the aftermath of war. (Grades 5-7)

Mattingley, Christobel. *The Miracle Tree*. Illustrated by Marianne Yamaguchi. San Diego: Harcourt Brace Jovanovich, 1985.
After the war, a young Japanese soldier searches for his beautiful bride in Nagasaki. An old woman searches for her missing daughter. A woman who was severely disfigured by the Nagasaki atom bomb watches from the window of her convalescent room as the former soldier, now a gardener, plants a pine tree on Christmas Day and tends it to maturity. She watches the old woman who comes twice a year to see how the tree grows and to remember her daughter. At last, 20 years after the tree was planted, the three are united in the miracle they had all been hoping for. (Grades 5-7)

McSwigan, Marie. *Snow Treasure*. Illustrated by Andre LaBlanc. New York: Dutton, 1942; Scholastic, n.d.
A group of children help Norwegian resistance workers smuggle $9,000,000 in gold bullion out of the country under the noses of Nazi sentries by hiding it on their sleds. (Grades 4-6)

Merrill, Jean. *The Pushcart War*. Illustrated by Ronni Solbert. Reading, MA: Addison-Wesley, 1964; Dell, 1987.

In this extremely funny satire about urban traffic problems, the pushcart peddlers of New York City declare war on the mammoth trucks—and win, through a combination of clever strategy and effective tactics. (Grades 5-8)

Morpurgo, Michael. *Waiting for Anya*. New York: Viking, 1991.

Young Jo risks his life to help protect the Jewish children who are trying to flee from Vichy France into Spain. Eventually, the whole village gets involved; even the German corporal colludes in their escape. Similar in theme and plot to Claire Hachet Bishop's *Twenty and Ten*, this will appeal to slightly older readers. (Grades 5-8)

Mukerji, Dhan Gopal. *Gay-Neck: The Story of a Pigeon*. Illustrated by Boris Artzybasheff. New York: Dutton, 1927.

This early Newbery award winner is rarely read by contemporary children. The slow pace of the narrative and the descriptive prose style are nearly insurmountable barriers to children unaccustomed to this discursive approach. Therefore, most child readers today will miss a powerful anti-war episode in which Gay-Neck is trained to be a carrier pigeon for Indian troops during World War I. Teachers might want to try reading aloud the passage in which Gay-Neck describes his experiences trying to fly ". . .through a million shuttles of flame, weaving the garment of red destruction on the loom of life" (p. 136). (Grades 5-8)

O'Dell, Scott. *Sarah Bishop*. New York: Houghton Mifflin, 1980.

Because Sarah's father is loyal to the British, he is the target of a raid by Birdsall's raiders and dies after being tarred and feathered. Her brother has joined the patriots and dies on a British prison ship. Sarah survives the War for Independence on her own, supported by her musket and a fierce sense of autonomy. (Grades 6-9)

———. *Sing Down the Moon*. Boston: Houghton Mifflin, 1970.

This novel chronicles the forced 300-mile Long Walk of the Navahos from their home in the Canyon de Chelly to Fort Sumner in 1863. It is just one more tragic incident in the Indian wars fought by the United States government against the nations who occupied the land first. (Grades 6-8)

Oneal, Zibby. *War Work*. Illustrated by George Porter. New York: Viking, 1971.

Three young children in a Midwestern town have collected tin cans, rubber scrap, and old grease, and they've weeded their victory garden. Their war work involves them in a sinister mystery, however, when they start to track down a spy network. The mystery is not very convincing, but the children are engaging, and their responses to World War II seem appropriately childlike. (Grades 4-6)

Orgel, Doris. *A Certain Magic*. New York: Dial, 1976.

Jenny knows she shouldn't be doing it, but she is unable to resist reading her Aunt Trudl's copybook, the diary of the time just before World War II that she spent with a British family after being sent from Vienna. Full of secrets she shouldn't know, Jenny goes off to England for a holiday with her parents and tracks down the daughter of that British family. Finding herself in possession of the emerald that held a certain magic for Trudl, half evil and half good, she tries to exorcize those demons and make peace with Aunt Trudl and the past. World War II, with its terrors for European Jews, is part of the backdrop but not as central as it is in the author's *The Devil in Vienna*. (Grades 4-6)

————. *The Devil in Vienna*. New York: Dial, 1978.

In Vienna in 1938, a Jewish girl and the daughter of a Nazi official struggle to retain their friendship while Hitler takes over Austria. Based on the author's own experiences, the novel is a poignant account of how children's lives can be affected by the political beliefs of their parents. (Grades 5-8)

Orlev, Uri. *The Island on Bird Street*. Translated from the Hebrew by Hillel Halkin. Boston: Houghton Mifflin, 1984.

Eleven-year-old Alex hides out in an abandoned building in the Warsaw Ghetto after his father is taken away by the German army. This is a well-written, haunting survival story as well as a testament to the strength of family ties. (Grades 5-8)

————. *The Man from the Other Side*. Translated from the Hebrew by Hillel Halkin. Boston: Houghton Mifflin, 1991.

A Polish boy gains a new understanding of the Jews enclosed in the Warsaw Ghetto when he learns that his own father, persecuted as a Communist, was a Jew. Based on a true story. (Grades 6-8)

Paterson, Katherine. *Park's Quest*. New York: Dutton, 1988.

Parkington Waddell Broughton the Fifth is 11 years old and dreams of a past and a future that would be worthy of his splendid name. Clouding his past is the mystery of his father who died in Vietnam before Park was born, a father his mother refuses to discuss. When Park finally visits his paternal grandfather's farm in Virginia, he learns far more than he expected to about his father and his father's family. While this is primarily Park's story, his newly discovered half-sister Than plays another important role and gives a rare dimension to a young reader's understanding of the significance of the Vietnam War to the United States. Use this sensitive, well-written novel with *Charlie Pippin* by Candy Boyd, another story about a young adolescent's quest to understand the meaning of the Vietnam War in her father's life. (Grades 5-8)

Pearson, Kit. *The Sky Is Falling*. New York: Viking, 1989.

Norah and her little brother have been evacuated from England to Canada in the summer of 1940. Stubborn and proud, Norah doesn't seem to fit in at school or at home with the two wealthy women who have taken the children in. Her growing self-awareness and her accommodation to the situation are convincing. (Grades 5-7)

Prince, Alison. *How's Business*. New York: Four Winds, 1987.

In a plot that is similar to Streatfeild's *When the Sirens Wailed*, Howard Grainger leaves the safety of Aunt Kath's home, to which he has been evacuated, to return to London because he is worried about his mother. (Grades 4-6)

Reeder, Carolyn. *Shades of Gray*. New York: Macmillan, 1989.

Left an orphan after the Civil War, twelve-year-old Will Page is sent to live with his aunt whose husband, Uncle Jed, had refused to fight for the Confederacy. Will learns a great deal about himself and about the true meaning of courage and honor as he comes to understand why his uncle opposed the war. A thought-provoking book. (Grades 6-8)

Reiss, Johanna. *The Upstairs Room*. New York: Crowell, 1972.

Annie and her big sister Sini are hidden from the Nazis for more than two years by a kind Dutch farm family. Inevitably compared with Anne Frank's diary, this autobiographical novel has its own poignant story to tell. Its sequel, *The Journey Back*, is the equally eloquent account of the difficult adjustment to postwar life by one Jewish family in Holland. (Grades 5-8)

Richter, Hans Peter. *Friedrich*. Translated from the German by Edite Kroll. New York: Holt, 1970.

A young German boy tells the story of his best friend whose fate is representative of most of the Jews living under the Nazi regime. Beginning in 1929, the year of their birth, the anti-Semitic attitudes and policies lead inexorably to Friedrich's death in 1942. (Grades 6-8)

————. *I Was There*. Translated from the German by Edite Kroll. New York: Holt, 1972; Puffin, 1987.

In this companion to *Friedrich*, we see more clearly the day-to-day events in the life of a young boy moving through the ranks of the *Jungvolk*, graduating to the Hitler Youth, and finally ending in combat with the German troops on the eastern front. The author writes that in this novel he is reporting what he saw because he was there, that he believed it all then—and will never believe again. (Grades 6-8)

Roth-Hano, Renee. *Touch Wood: A Girlhood in Occupied France*. New York: Four Winds, 1988.

Her parents have fled from Hungary to Alsace and now to Paris, looking for a safe place for a Jewish family to live. Renee's diary records the mounting persecution of Jews in Paris until finally her parents send her and her two little sisters to a Catholic convent in Normandy for safety. The girls are treated kindly there, although they become understandably confused about their religious identity. They survive the intense bombings when the Allies land and return to Paris after the war to be reunited with their parents. The happy ending in this autobiographical novel will be welcomed by young readers although adults will recognize that Renee was one of the few lucky Jewish survivors. (Grades 5-7)

Rylant, Cynthia. *A Blue-Eyed Daisy*. New York: Bradbury, 1985.

This episodic novel covers a year in the life of Ellie Farley, who lives with her parents, four sisters, and a dog named Bullet in a coal mining town in West Virginia. In one episode, "Uncle Joe," Ellie's favorite uncle joins the Air Force and gets sent to Vietnam. He comes home on leave and seems a foot taller and nearly as old as her father. He doesn't talk about the war, so nobody else does either. It bothers Ellie; she has questions she wants to ask him. But one night she watches him watching the late news on television, listening to the reports of dead soldiers; now he looks as old as her grandfather, and he is crying. (Grades 5-8)

Sachs, Marilyn. *A Pocket Full of Seeds.* Illustrated by Ben Stahl. New York: Doubleday, 1973.

Through the eyes of a young girl who is Jewish as well as French, we see the Nazi horror spread through Europe from 1938 to 1943. Nicole's family is taken away by the German soldiers, and she hides with the school mistress who shelters her with false identity papers but little love. Some young readers will be dismayed with the ending, which leaves Nicole still uncertain that she will ever see her parents again; but that was the reality of World War II for many children. (Grades 4-7)

Serraillier, Ian. *The Silver Sword.* Illustrated by C. Walter Hodges. New York: Criterion, 1960.

When the German soldiers take their parents away, the Balicki children must live on their own in war-torn Poland. This is the story of their day-to-day survival, their flight across Europe as refugees after the war, and their ultimate reunion with their mother and father in Switzerland. (Grades 5-7)

Service, Pamela F. *Winter of Magic's Return.* New York: Atheneum, 1985.

Five hundred years after a nuclear holocaust and nuclear winter have devastated the land and people of Britain, two children, Wellington and Heather, join forces with Merlin, who has been resurrected as a gawky teenager. They find Arthur and save their land from dark magical forces. Wellington had dreamed of creating wonders of strategic warfare until he learns that it was a fascination with strategy and technology for its own sake that had caused the nuclear disaster which threw his country back to the Stone Age. (Grades 5-7)

Shemin, Margaretha. *The Empty Moat.* New York: Coward-McCann, 1969.

An aristocratic young Dutch girl whose family castle is occupied by German soldiers is at first convinced that she must put her family interests first and take no personal risks that would endanger her invalid father. As the war progresses, however, she comes to see the importance of resistance and finds the courage to participate. (Grades 6-8)

————. *The Little Riders.* Illustrated by Peter Spier. New York: Coward-McCann, 1963.

An American girl is stranded at her Dutch grandparents' home in Alkmaar when the German army invades Holland. She hates the invading soldiers who prevent her from being reunited with her parents for more than four years. She learns to see the human being behind one Nazi uniform, however, when the German officer who is quartered in their home helps her hide the 12 little riders, the beloved lead figures from the town's clock tower that the Germans want to melt down for munitions. (Grades 4-6)

Singer, Isaac Bashevis. "The Power of Light," in *The Power of Light: Eight Stories for Hanukkah.* Illustrated by Irene Lieblich. New York: Farrar Straus Giroux, 1980.

> The title story in this collection is a reminiscence about the Hanukkah spent by two teenagers hiding out in the ruins of the burned-out Warsaw Ghetto, just before they escape to join the partisans. (Grades 6-8)

Smith, Doris Buchanan. *The First Hard Times.* New York: Viking, 1983.

> Ancil's mother has remarried, and her sisters are adjusting to the new stepfather with no difficulty. Ancil, however, is convinced that her father, who has been missing in action in Vietnam for 10 years, is still alive and that he deserves her undivided loyalty. (Grades 5-7)

Sorenson, Virginia. *Miracles on Maple Hill.* Illustrated by Beth and Joe Krush. New York: Harcourt Brace Jovanovich, 1956.

> In this Newbery Medal winner, a family is renewed by their move to a country farm house. The family member most in need of renewal is the father, traumatized by his experiences as a prisoner of war. The point of view is that of the twelve-year-old daughter, who rejoices in the slow recovery of his nerves and his optimism, as well as in the wonders of life in maple sugar country. (Grades 5-7)

Stiles, Martha Bennett. *Darkness Over the Land.* New York: Dial, 1966.

> A young German boy muddles through World War II, confused and torn between loyalty to the regime and loyalty to his parents who quietly oppose Hitler's policies. When the war ends, he is stricken with guilt and must reconcile his German identity with his knowledge of German wartime atrocities. This would be more convincing if the characters were more skillfully developed. (Grades 6-8)

Streatfeild, Noel. *When the Sirens Wailed.* Illustrated by Judith Gwyn Brown. New York: Random, 1976.

> Three working-class children who are evacuated from London at the beginning of the Blitz run away from an unpleasant billet only to find that their former home has been destroyed and their mother is missing. The story is marred by the patronizing tone and the author's tendency to introduce explanatory passages. (Grades 4-6)

Streiber, Whitley. *Wolf of Shadows.* New York: Knopf, 1985.

> A human mother and her daughter join a band of wolves and struggle to survive the nuclear winter after a nuclear war. The description of devastation to both human civilization and the natural environment is uncompromising, and the bond between the animal and human survivors is touching. A novel of impressive power and simplicity. (Grades 6+)

Sullivan, Mary Ann. *Child of War.* New York: Holiday House, 1984.

> This novel takes place in contemporary Belfast and deals with the effect of "The Troubles" on one thirteen-year-old Catholic girl. Her mother died fighting for the IRA, and now her little brother dies in Maeve's arms, shot by a British soldier. She becomes a rebel child for awhile, seeking revenge for her brother's

death, but finally loses her grasp on reality, maddened by guilt and grief. Young readers may find Maeve's breakdown puzzling or upsetting; it is inadequately prepared for in the narrative. This is, however, one of the very few books for young people about the civil war in Northern Ireland. (Grades 6-8)

Swindells, Robert. *Brother in the Land.* New York: Holiday House, 1985.
A teenage boy tells what it is like to be a survivor of a nuclear war that has devastated England. The portrayal of effects of radioactive fallout and the climatic changes of nuclear winter are downplayed here in favor of an emphasis on the changes in human behavior. (Grades 6-9)

Tomlinson, Theresa. *Summer Witches.* New York: Macmillan, 1991.
Two contemporary English girls create a secret meeting place out of the old air-raid shelter in Sarah's backyard. They find a strange note and mysterious paintings on the wall that lead them to discoveries and better feelings about the neighborhood "witch," an eccentric, deaf old lady who had been a little girl using the air-raid shelter during World War II when a bomb killed her mother. (Grades 4-6)

Travers, P.L. *I Go by Sea, I Go by Land.* New York: Norton, 1964.
This reprint of a 1941 title by the author of *Mary Poppins* reads today like propaganda for the British evacuation effort. Written in diary form, it tells the story of eleven-year-old Sabrina and her eight-year-old brother's voyage to the United States as part of the voluntary evacuation effort. These upper-class children experience no hardships en route or after they settle with equally upper-class relatives near New York City. Their worries about their parents and family home in England are far less prominent than their delight with the new experiences they are having. Evidently intended to show British children at their plucky best, the story suffers from implausible character development and the intrusion of the adult author's arch and knowing voice into what is meant to be a child's diary. This is useful today primarily as an example of wartime publishing for children. (Grades 4-7)

Treece, Henry. *The Invaders.* Illustrated by Charles Keeping. New York: Crowell, 1972.
Three short stories portray battles that occurred during the Roman, Viking, and Norman invasions of Britain. The battles are bloody, but they are far from heroic. These are stories about war that carry a profound plea for peace. (Grades 6-8)

———. *The Last Viking.* Illustrated by Charles Keeping. New York: Pantheon, 1966.
The Viking king Harald Hardrada met his death in 1066, fighting for the crown of England. It is a great death, according to the standards of warrior-heroes. Feeling that an arrow has dealt him a mortal blow to his throat, he croaks out a request to see the deadly weapon. A British carl puts it in his hand. Harald examines it and whispers, "The man who made this knew his trade" (p. 145). The Viking's life before this final battle is told in a series of flashbacks, and nobody does this kind of thing better than Henry Treece. (Grades 6-8)

————. *The Windswept City: A Novel of the Trojan War*. Illustrated by Faith Jaques. New York: Meredith, 1967.

> The culmination of the 10-year Trojan War is seen through the eyes of young Asterius, Helen's slave. (Grades 6-8)

Treseder, Terry Walton. *Hear O Israel: A Story of the Warsaw Ghetto*. Illustrated by Lloyd Bloom. New York: Atheneum, 1990.

> This short, handsomely designed book tells the story of the fate of the Warsaw Jews during World War II by presenting one family's experience. The book is poetic and powerful, communicating the impact of the Holocaust in a visceral way that the mere recounting of the facts sometimes misses. (Grades 5-8)

Uchida, Yoshiko. *Journey to Topaz: A Story of the Japanese-American Evacuation*. Berkeley, CA: Creative Arts, 1985.

> An autobiographical account of one Japanese-American family's experience as forced evacuees from their home in California to a concentration camp in Utah. Vivid in its details about camp life, the novel succeeds in presenting both the personal and political consequences of President Roosevelt's executive order 9066. *Journey Home*, the sequel, portrays the family's efforts to recreate a normal life after the crushing internment experience is over. (Grades 6-8)

Van Stockum, Hilda. *The Borrowed House*. New York: Farrar Straus Giroux, 1975.

> Janna is the twelve-year-old daughter of a German theatrical couple who have "borrowed" the home of a wealthy Dutch family in Amsterdam during the German occupation in Holland. Slowly, Janna comes to understand that she has been taught lies about Hitler and the war which Germany is waging and even helps a Jewish boy who is hidden in the house. Her conversion may be unconvincing, but this provides yet another perspective on World War II. (Grades 5-7)

————. *The Winged Watchman*. New York: Farrar, Straus & Giroux, 1962.

> The hardships of war are not sugar-coated in this story about the German occupation of Holland. There is death and starvation as well as heroism and resistance. The Verhagen family may seem almost too noble to be believed, but they are likable and interesting with their home in a working windmill. (Grades 4-6)

Voigt, Cynthia. *Tree by Leaf*. New York: Atheneum, 1988.

> Clothilde's father has come home from World War I with a face so disfigured and a soul so disheartened that he refuses to enter the family home and stays in the boathouse, a silent recluse. In this time of serious family difficulties, no one is able to guide Clothilde until she hears a voice that asks her what she wants. Clothilde learns much about answered prayers, the horrid legacy of war, her family, and herself in this challenging, rewarding novel. (Grades 6-9)

Vos, Ida. *Hide and Seek*. Translated from the Dutch by Terese Edelstein and Inez Smidt. Boston: Houghton Mifflin, 1991.

> A novel about childhood years spent hiding from the Nazis in Holland. Childlike in its simplicity and apparent bewilderment at events spinning out of control,

this novel will help even young children to understand why little Esther is still afraid to play outside and Rachel's grandfather steals food even after the war is over. An afterword pays tribute to the 100,000 Dutch Jews who died in German concentration camps. (Grades 4-6)

Walsh, Jill Paton. *The Dolphin Crossing*. New York: Dell, 1990.

Two teenage boys, an evacuee from a London slum and the son of a privileged country family, overcome their initial distrust of each other and find that they share similar ideas about the war. Frustrated because they are too young to fight, they join in the great effort to evacuate British soldiers from Dunkirk. It's a great adventure story and a fine account of the blurring of class lines that sometimes occurred during World War II. (Grades 6-8)

Wartski, Maureen Crane. *A Boat to Nowhere*. Illustrated by Dick Teicher. Louisville, KY: Westminster, 1980.

Three children and an old man flee in a small fishing boat from threatening government officials in post-war Vietnam. The narrative leading to the family's escape from Vietnam is stilted and didactic, but the description of their experiences as boat people is dramatic and convincing. (Grades 6-8)

Watkins, Yoko Kawashima. *So Far from the Bamboo Grove*. New York: Lothrop, 1986; Puffin, 1987.

When World War II ends, eleven-year-old Yoko, her mother, and older sister must find their way from their home in northern Korea near their father's place of business in Manchuria back to Japan. It is a hard, dangerous journey, made more difficult by the hostility of many Koreans, especially the North Korean Communist army, to the Japanese who had forcibly occupied their country. The hardships of the women are not over when they reach Japan. They are now refugees with few resources for starting a new life in the defeated, war-torn country. This autobiographical novel conveys both the toughness and sweetness that enabled the sisters to survive, even after the death of their mother. (Grades 6-8)

Werstein, Irving. *The Long Escape*. New York: Scribner, 1964.

A prologue sets the historical stage for the German invasion of Belgium in 1940. The novel then turns to Justine Raymond, the director of a convalescent home for 50 children, who manages to bring them to safety in England just ahead of the advancing German troops. While the story has much dramatic potential, its adult protagonist will not be very interesting to most young readers; her determination is heroic but ultimately less compelling than the experiences of the children under her charge, and we learn very little about them. (Grades 5-7)

Westall, Robert. *The Kingdom by the Sea*. New York: Farrar Straus Giroux, 1991.

Twelve-year-old Harry takes off on his own after he survives a bombing raid that destroys his home in northern England. He "sleeps rough" on the coast, accompanied by a dog who is also the lone survivor of a Luftwaffe attack. He seems to bring out both the best and worst in the adults he encounters along the way, all of whom seem to have an empty "boy-sized place" in their lives. (There is a particularly unsavory incident with a homosexual British corporal.) This is ultimately a story of survival and growing self-awareness, with the attention to detail and vivid writing one expects of Westall. (Grades 6-8)

Wibberley, Leonard. *John Treegate's Musket.* New York: Farrar, Straus and Cudahy, 1959.

This first volume of a series about the American Revolution traces the events from 1769 to 1775 which resulted in John Treegate's conversion from loyal supporter of the king to armed participant against the British in the Battle of Bunker Hill. Besides the unusually clear and objective presentation of political issues of the time, this is a wonderful adventure story, tracing the escapades of John's son Peter from his unwitting involvement in a murder, to his escape from Boston on a ship illegally doing trade in the West Indies, to his shipwreck in a hurricane, to his rescue by a Scottish man living in the Carolina mountains. (Grades 6-8)

Wisler, G. Clifton. *Red Cap.* New York: Lodestar/Dutton, 1991.

The author has based his novel on records of an actual thirteen-year-old Union drummer boy who was imprisoned in the infamous Confederate prison at Andersonville. His plucky determination to live up to his military obligations and his small stature seem to have won the protection and friendship of Confederate as well as Union soldiers. Serving as the camp drummer boy, Ransom J. Powell was the only member of his nineteen-man company to survive the horrors of Andersonville and be released to the North in an exchange of prisoners in 1864. (Grades 6-8)

Yep, Laurence. *The Serpent's Children.* New York: Harper & Row, 1984.

Cassia's father has devoted his life to fighting the Manchus and has also tried to fight off the British invaders. Cassia is no less a warrior, fighting off hunger, bandits, and convention. Her brother's battles are different yet and take him eventually to a new life in California. This is a fine historical novel, set against the winds of social change blowing across China in the nineteenth century. (Grades 6-8)

Yolen, Jane. *The Devil's Arithmetic.* New York: Viking, 1988; Puffin, 1990.

Through the magic of time travel, a contemporary American Jewish girl finds herself in a Polish village in 1940. When Nazi soldiers take her to a concentration camp, she learns first-hand the horrors which her family in New Rochelle had urged her never to forget. (Grades 5-7)

Zei, Alki. *Petros' War.* Translated from the Greek by Edward Fenton. New York: Holt, 1968.

As a ten-year-old boy in occupied Athens, Petros doesn't feel that he has contributed much to the Resistance; all he has done is liberate a dog from a cruel German soldier and paint slogans on the wall. Then he sees two of his best friends shot, and the slogan "Freedom or Death" acquires new meaning for him. (Grades 5-7)

————. *Wildcat Under Glass*. Translated from the Greek by Edward Fenton. New York: Holt, 1968.

Two Greek sisters watch differences in political ideology cause tensions in their family and in their society as a fascist regime takes over. A good child's perspective on important European events that preceded World War II. (Grades 4-6)

Fiction for Young Adults

Aaron, Chester. *Gideon*. New York: Lippincott, 1982.

Gideon survives his first early adolescent years in the Warsaw Ghetto by acquiring a tough cynicism and essential survival skills. Rejecting his parents' moral position, he collaborates with Polish thugs and operates a successful smuggling enterprise. When his father kills himself and a German soldier to spare Gideon's own life, he begins to participate actively in the resistance movement, fighting to the last days of the Uprising. He escapes through the sewer to join a partisan band, but he is betrayed and sent to Treblinka. Still determined to survive, he is one of the few Jews to escape in the rebellion that occurred just before the liberation of that concentration camp. Now he is writing the story down for his wife and children, trying to regain his memories and his identity as a Jew. The events in this story are powerful and compelling, and Gideon is an interesting character whose motivations are unfortunately often as opaque to the reader as they are to him. (Grades 7-9)

Adams, Richard. *Watership Down*. New York: Macmillan, 1974.

This is an animal fantasy about a group of rabbits who set out to find a new home. Much of the adventure involves a violent struggle with a group of enemy rabbits. The military tactics are intricate, and the battles are truly ferocious. (Grades 7+)

Alexander, Lloyd. *The Kestrel*. New York: Dutton, 1982; Dell, 1983.

In this sequel to *Westmark*, war comes to the kingdom, and Theo and Mickle test their values and their love against a background of bloodshed. This is superb fantasy, full of adventure, humor, and complex ideas. The reader comes to see the folly and horror of war through Theo's eyes, as Mickle grows accomplished in the art of diplomacy. This is a sophisticated plea for peace among nations as well as a finely wrought young adult novel. (Grades 7-10)

Bedard, Michael. *Redwork*. New York: Atheneum, 1990.

A fifteen-year-old boy is strangely drawn to the the old man who lives downstairs, until he finds himself experiencing World War I battles that Mr. Magnus had fought in, even wounding the same leg that Mr. Magnus lost in the war. Young Cass and his friend Maddy befriend the old man who is haunting Cass's dreams and learn about alchemy, growing old, and the power of human kindness. A strange and wonderful novel. (Grades 8-10)

Benard, Robert, editor. *A Short Wait Between Trains: An Anthology of War Short Stories by American Writers*. New York: Delacorte, 1991.

Twenty-two selections are included in this anthology of short stories about war by major American authors, including Eudora Welty, Ernest Hemingway, William Faulkner, Philip Roth, and Tim O'Brien. A stronger editorial hand, including introductory material setting each story in context, would have made this collection more accessible to the young readers for whom it is intended. (Grades 9+)

Benchley, Nathaniel. *Bright Candles: A Novel of the Danish Resistance*. New York: Harper & Row, 1974.

Sixteen-year-old Jens Hansen tells how he and his friends worked with the Resistance against the Germans who occupied their country in 1940. There is little character development or tension in the narrative; what is important are the events themselves. (Grades 8-10)

————. *Only Earth and Sky Last Forever*. New York: Harper & Row, 1972.

Dark Elk longs to prove himself as a warrior and win Lashuka as his bride. He joins up with Crazy Horse and participates in the Battle of the Little Bighorn, only to have Lashuka die at the white man's hand. (Grades 7-9)

Briggs, Raymond. *The Tin-Pot Foreign General and the Old Iron Woman*. Boston: Little, Brown, 1984.

This picture book for grown-ups is Briggs' critique of the Falklands War, an episode which few young adults will remember. The caricature of Margaret Thatcher is devastating, and the anti-war message is unmistakable. (Grades 7+)

————. *When the Wind Blows*. New York: Schocken, 1982.

In a comic strip format, Briggs tells the story of the elderly British couple who dutifully follow the government's civil defense procedures when a nuclear bomb lands in England. This is a devastating attack on the notion that a nuclear war is survivable. (Grades 7+)

Burton, Hestor. *In Spite of All Terror*. Illustrated by Victor G. Ambrus. New York: World, 1968.

1940 was the year that Churchill called on all civilian Britons to actively support the war effort. That year is seen through the eyes of a fifteen-year-old evacuee from London to the small village of Chiddingford. The high point of the novel is Dunkirk. Liz, a mere girl, is barred from helping on their small boat by Ben and old General Brereton, but she does her part on shore, helping the rescued British soldiers send telegrams to their families and friends. The plot has little direction or tension; this novel tells its story through an accumulation of small incidents and observations. (Grades 7-9)

Bykov, Vasil. *Pack of Wolves*. Translated from the Russian by Lynn Solotaroff. New York: Crowell, 1981.

This is the story of two days in Russia during World War II. A small group of Russian soldiers has been encircled by German troops. Levchuk is ordered to take some of their wounded, including a female radio operator who is due to give birth, to a nearby medical unit. The story of Levchuk and the baby should be more compelling than it is. Unfortunately, the turgid prose style fails to carry the narrative. (Grades 8-10)

Clapp, Patricia. *I'm Deborah Sampson: A Soldier in the War of the Revolution*. New York: Lothrop, Lee & Shepard, 1977.
This fictionalized biography provides Deborah Sampson with a motive for disguising herself as a young man and joining the Continental Army. It also provides answers for questions that many young people will have about how she got away with her disguise in the crowded intimacy of military life. (Grades 7-9)

―――. *The Tamarack Tree*. New York: Lothrop, Lee & Shepard, 1986.
Brought to Vicksburg, Mississippi, from England in 1859 by her older brother, Rosemary is just beginning to enjoy the pleasures of a young Southern lady when the Civil War begins. Torn between her anti-slavery ideals and her affections for the Southerners she has come to know, she endures the siege of Vicksburg and sees the war finally come to an end. She observes her brother's romance with a Vicksburg belle crumbling because of their differing views on slavery, helps nurse the wounded Confederate soldiers, enjoys the devotion of a Yankee cartographer, and finally returns to England both saddened and enriched by her years in a turbulent, war-torn land. (Grades 8-10)

Cohen, Daniel. *The Ghosts of War*. New York: Putnam, 1990.
These short, easy-reading "true" ghost stories with war themes, including haunted battlefields and soldiers' premonitions of death, may lead reluctant readers to other meatier accounts. Some of these also lend themselves to telling or reading aloud and could be used by a librarian or teacher to introduce other books. (Grades 7-9)

Collier, James Lincoln, and Christopher Collier. *The Bloody Country*. New York: Macmillan, 1976.
Using their typical formula, the authors present historical events of the Revolutionary War era from the perspective of a young boy. This time the focus is on a massacre of civilians by the British and their Indian allies at the end of the Revolutionary War and on a conflict over disputed land between Connecticut and Pennsylvania. In both cases, it is women and children who bear the brunt of the suffering. (Grades 7-9)

―――. *My Brother Sam Is Dead*. New York: Four Winds, 1974.
Tim Meeker watches the confrontation between his Tory father and his Patriot brother, a confrontation that becomes meaningless when both are killed in absurd episodes of the Revolutionary War. This well-written novel presents the ambiguity of a war fought for ideological reasons. (Grades 7-9)

―――. *The Winter Hero*. New York: Macmillan, 1978.
After the War for Independence, the young nation suffered growing pains for many years. In Massachusetts, many people who had fought for independence now found their state government nearly as oppressive as the British had been. Shays' Rebellion was the result. The story of that abortive revolution is told

from the point of view of a boy who had been too young to fight in the Revolution and who now yearns to prove himself a hero in this mini-war. (Grades 7-9)

Cormier, Robert. *After the First Death.* New York: Pantheon, 1979; Dell, 1991.

Terrorists take a bus of school children hostage, and a general's son is sent to them as a messenger. The aftermath of violence leaves no one untouched. A disturbing, ambiguous novel for thoughtful adolescents to ponder. (Grades 8-10)

Crew, Linda. *Children of the River.* New York: Delacorte, 1989.

Sundara had escaped from the Khmer Rouge in Cambodia with her aunt's family four years ago when she was thirteen. Now she attends an Oregon high school and feels that she doesn't fit in anywhere; she is too Cambodian for her peers at school and too American for her family at home. The novel is about her efforts to deal with her new life in the United States, her painful memories of loved ones she may never see again, and her guilt at having survived. (Grades 7-10)

Emerson, Zack. *Welcome to Vietnam.* New York: Scholastic, 1991.

This is the first volume in the paperback Echo Company series about combat in Vietnam. The approach is similar to that used by Walter Myers in *Fallen Angels*, presenting the war through the eyes of a representative group of young soldiers; but the writing is far more formulaic and pedestrian. If you buy this in a bookstore, it comes shrink-wrapped with a metal dog tag which makes a very nice book mark. (Grades 8-10)

Ferry, Charles. *Raspberry One.* New York: Houghton Mifflin, 1983.

The author says he wrote this novel to help make sense of his own wartime experiences, and there is a tone of introspective nostalgia to this story about two members of a torpedo squadron during World War II. Their initial idealism and desire for heroic deeds are sorely tested by the reality of bloody, costly battles in the Pacific. One man loses a hand; the other has a badly damaged knee. They seem strangely untouched by their experiences, however, just relieved to have come out of it alive. (Grades 8-10)

Forbes, Esther. *Johnny Tremain.* Illustrated by Lynd Ward. New York: Houghton Mifflin, 1943; Yearling, 1987.

Revolutionary Boston is seen through the eyes of young Johnny Tremain. When a bad burn cripples his hand, he must abandon a promising career as a silversmith. He becomes a courier for a printer and gets swept up in the ideas and adventure of the Whig resistance to the British. Here is a rich historical novel that makes the events of the Boston Tea Party, the Battle of Lexington, and Paul Revere's ride come alive as the exciting backdrop of one young man's life. (Grades 7+)

Forman, James. *Ceremony of Innocence.* New York: Hawthorn, 1970.

A fictionalized account of the White Rose resistance movement, told primarily in flashbacks as Hans Scholl, arrested and imprisoned by the Nazis, remembers the events that led him and his sister Sophie to start writing and distributing anti-Nazi leaflets. (Grades 7-9)

————. *The Cow Neck Rebels*. New York: Farrar Straus & Giroux, 1969.
Young Bruce Cameron loses his innocence and his taste for war after being tried in battle in 1776. This novel includes one of the most realistic and repellent death scenes in young adult literature, as Malcolm Cameron's mortal wound festers and swarms with maggots in the sweltering August heat of the Battle of Long Island. (Grades 7-9)

————. *A Fine, Soft Day*. New York: Farrar Straus Giroux, 1978.
The main plot involves Brian O'Brien and his family in Belfast. Brian's older brother is a member of the Provos, a militant wing of the IRA; his sister works for peace. Brian just wants to hold the family together. A subplot traces a machine gun from its use by an American soldier in the attack on My Lai in Vietnam to its use on the streets of Belfast. (Grades 7-9)

————. *Horses of Anger*. New York: Farrar Straus & Giroux, 1967.
The author tries to portray the disillusionment of young German soldiers at the end of World War II who are assigned to man flak guns whose range cannot possibly reach the American bombers. Flashbacks contrast the rhetoric and propaganda of the early days of Hitler's rule with the harsh reality of its final days. (Grades 8-10)

————. *My Enemy, My Brother*. New York: Meredith, 1969.
A young survivor of the Nazi concentration camps who craves peace makes his way to Palestine only to discover that war and conflict with their Arab neighbors is the Israeli promise of the future. (Grades 8-10)

————. *Prince Charlie's Year*. New York: Scribner's, 1991.
Colin MacDonald, on his way to fight with the Patriots against the British in 1780, remembers another war when he fought with the Highland troops in the Jacobite struggle to place Bonnie Prince Charlie on the British throne. That was a disillusioning experience, but he hopes that this war will bring the freedom that was denied him as a young man. (Grades 7-10)

Frank, Rudolf. *No Hero for the Kaiser*. Translated from the German by Patricia Crampton. Illustrated by Klaus Steffens. New York: Lothrop, Lee & Shepard, 1986.
The author intended this to be "an anti-war novel to warn young people." First published in Germany in 1931, it chronicles life in the German army from the point of view of a young Polish boy who is the sole survivor of an attack on his village by both Russian and German troops. He is adopted by a German battery and becomes an honorary soldier, experiencing first-hand the drudgery, pain, and bloodshed of military life. In the ironic ending, Jan runs away to avoid being made a symbol of wartime heroism by the Kaiser. This will be difficult reading for most contemporary young people, with its somewhat dated style and labored translation, as well as allusions to unfamiliar European landmarks and historical events. (Grades 9-12)

Fritz, Jean. *Early Thunder*. Illustrated by Lynd Ward. New York: Coward-McCann, 1967; Puffin, 1987.

At 14, Daniel West is a fervent Tory, like the rest of his family. As events progress during the stormy months of 1775, however, he makes a decision to join the Whigs in opposing the English. This novel successfully captures both the ideological and personal conflicts that dominated life in places like Salem, Massachusetts, in the period just before the American Revolution. (Grades 7-10)

Gardam, Jane. *A Long Way from Verona*. New York: Macmillan, 1971.

At 13, Jessica Vye is bright, introspective, independent, and often combative. England is at war, and it touches Jessica in strange ways. A first date with a boy who takes her to the slums to see social injustice with her own eyes is interrupted by a bombing raid that seems to level gaps between people even as it levels buildings. A chance encounter with an escaped Italian prisoner becomes a transcendental experience. A luminous, special novel. (Grades 7-10)

Garfield, Leon. *The Drummer Boy*. Illustrated by Anthony Maitland. New York: Pantheon, 1969.

A British drummer boy is haunted by the ghost of a soldier who died, not as a hero on the battlefield but as a victim of a freak accident in a barn. A typical Garfield novel, it makes no stylistic compromises for its intended young readers. Its rich, colloquial language, Dickensian characters, and twisting, dense plot will reward those who stick with it. (Grades 7-10)

Gehrts, Barbara. *Don't Say a Word*. Translated from the German by Elizabeth D. Crawford. New York: McElderry/Macmillan, 1986.

Anna's father is an officer in the Luftwaffe, but he works secretly against Hitler and is eventually sentenced to death for treason. An autobiographical novel about World War II in Germany, from the perspective of the Christian opposition. (Grades 7-9)

Greene, Bette. *Summer of My German Soldier*. New York: Dial, 1973; Bantam, 1974.

Twelve-year-old Patty Bergen is a Jewish girl living in a small town in Arkansas. Rejected and even abused by her parents, she is lonely and unsure of herself until she meets a German prisoner of war who has been sent to a camp near her home. Anton seems to see something special in her, and she develops a crush on him. When he escapes from the camp, she gives him fresh clothing as well as food and shelter for a few days in an abandoned garage behind her home. In a pivotal and moving scene at the center of the novel, Patty's father beats her with a belt as punishment for talking with a boy that he disapproves of. Anton rushes out from his hiding place to help her, but Patty warns him away. The moment is witnessed by Ruth, the black woman who cooks and cares for the Bergen household. Later she is able to reassure Patty that Anton had truly cared for her, that he was ready to risk his life for her. As the story unwinds, Anton is caught and killed, and Patty is sent to a reform school. The novel ends with Ruth, the only person to visit Patty in the reform school, leaving Patty alone. Patty is bereft, feeling as though her only life raft was floating away. "And yet somewhere in my mind's eye I thought I could see the faintest outline of land. Then it came to me that maybe that's the only thing life rafts are supposed to do. Taking the shipwrecked, not exactly to the land, but only in view of land. The final mile being theirs alone to swim" (p. 198). This deeply felt novel has been criticized for the stereotypical portrayal of Ruth, the strong, noble black servant; but since Ruth is viewed through Patty's eyes, this characterization seems appropriate. The irony of the Jewish girl helping a German prisoner is not overplayed; this is not so much a book about World War II in the United States as it is a story about a painful coming of age for an unhappy young girl. (Grades 7-9)

Hahn, Mary Downing. *December Stillness*. New York: Clarion, 1988; Avon, 1990.
A fifteen-year-old girl becomes obsessed with the local homeless man; she comes to see him as another casualty of the Vietnam War when he is killed by a car while walking along the highway with his ever-present plastic bags of belongings. When she and her father go together to the Vietnam Memorial, her father also begins to come to terms with his own Vietnam experience. (Grades 7-10)

Hall, Lynn. *If Winter Comes*. New York: Scribner's, 1986.
The United States faces an imminent nuclear attack by a small Latin American nation. We experience the threat of immediate or lingering death from nuclear fallout through the eyes of a teenage girl who wants desperately to live and her pessimistic boyfriend who looks for an excuse to die. The characterization and writing can't quite carry the weight of the theme, but this novel may stir thought and discussion among other young teenagers. (Grades 7-10)

Hansen, Joyce. *Which Way Freedom?* New York: Walker, 1986.
Obi escapes from the small farm where he was a slave and joins the Union Army, experiencing the bloody battle at Fort Pillow, Tennessee. (Grades 7-10)

Hartling, Peter. *Crutches*. Translated from the German by Elizabeth D. Crawford. New York: Lothrop, Lee & Shepard, 1988.
In the chaos immediately following World War II in Europe, a young boy and a crippled former Nazi soldier band together for survival. Their mutual need develops into affection and respect. The underlying theme of this novel is the ultimate triumph of humanity in the most dehumanizing times. (Grades 7-9)

Haugaard, Erik Christian. *Cromwell's Boy*. Boston: Houghton Mifflin, 1978.
This sequel to *A Messenger for Parliament* (Houghton Mifflin, 1976) continues the story of a young boy caught up in the British Civil War of the 1640s. These stories present war as a confusing and often senseless battle of competing religious and political ideologies in which the life of one individual doesn't count for much. This is one of the few novels for children in which the young protagonist actually kills on the battlefield. Readers may be surprised at his lack of reaction. This is difficult reading which presumes some familiarity with history and makes few concessions to conventional notions about what children need in a story. Even sophisticated young readers may be bothered by the abrupt

ending, which leaves many questions unanswered about Oliver's fate. (Grades 7-9)

Kassem, Lou. *Listen for Rachel*. New York: McElderry/Macmillan, 1986.
In this historical romance, the Civil War is secondary to the Tennessee mountain setting and the character development of the young heroine who learns self-worth as she acquires the healing lore of plants and herbs from an old mountain woman. (Grades 7-9)

Keith, Harold. *Rifles for Watie*. New York: Crowell, 1957; Harper, 1987.
This Newbery award winner tells the story of young Jefferson Davis Bussey, from his enlistment in Kansas in 1861 through his experiences in the Union infantry and cavalry, his 14 months as an undercover scout in the Confederate forces of Stand Watie, his falling in love with a Southern Cherokee girl, and his return to Kansas in 1865. Readers who stick it out through this long odyssey will gain an understanding of the impact of the Civil War on some of the Indian nations as well as the everyday life of a young soldier in that war. (Grades 7-10)

Kerr, M.E. *Gentlehands*. New York: Harper, 1978.
Events from World War II intrude into the present day in this novel for young adults. When Buddy Boyle falls in love with Skye Pennington, a year older and far wealthier and more worldly than he is, he introduces her to his grandfather. Grandfather Trenker is estranged from Buddy's family, but he is aristocratic and cultured and "European" enough to impress Skye and to help Buddy acquire some of the polish he thinks he needs to move in her circles. It all falls apart when an investigative journalist exposes Trenker as a Nazi war criminal, a notorious concentration camp official known as "Gentlehands" because of the Puccini aria he loved to play as he tortured his victims. Buddy must deal with his conflicted loyalties, his own sense of honor and identity, and his growing realization that his grandfather was indeed guilty of the crimes with which he has been charged. The Holocaust and anti-Semitism in the U.S. are integral elements of the plot in this well-written, accessible novel. (Grades 8-10)

Knowles, John. *A Separate Peace*. New York: Macmillan, 1960,
This novel about friendship and betrayal in an eastern prep school has become a young adult classic. Here World War II is presented as the looming destiny awaiting a group of young men as soon as they turn 18. (Grades 9-12)

Laird, Christa. *Shadow of the Wall*. New York: Greenwillow, 1989.
Misha is nearly 14, the age when residents of the Orphans' Home must leave to make their own way in the Warsaw Ghetto. This novel deals with his decision to join the young people who risk their lives to make contact with Jews in other parts of Poland. It also presents a fictional portrait of Janusz Korczak, a real-life hero. (Grades 7-9)

Lawrence, Louise. *Children of the Dust*. New York: Harper & Row, 1985.
The science fiction genre is used to present the new society which emerges after a nuclear holocaust. The new species which evolves is seen not as deformed mutants but rather as a more highly developed form of life than *homo sapiens*. (Grades 8-10)

Leffland, Ella. *Rumors of Peace*. New York: Harper, 1979.
Suse Hansen moves into adolescence in her small California town while World War II runs its course. Her preoccupation with the war is a constant through these years, as she discovers her intellectual powers, her sexuality, and her own place in the world. A satisfying and poignant novel about coming of age in a turbulent time, this could be seen as a female counterpoint to Knowles' *A Separate Peace*. (Grades 8-12)

Lisle, Janet Taylor. *Sirens and Spies*. New York: Bradbury, 1985.
Two sisters try to find out the truth about the wartime past of their exotic French violin teacher. One clue is the picture that Elsie finds in a book of photographs about World War II; it is definitely a young Miss Fitch, with her head shaved, carrying a baby, being carted through her French village while her neighbors jeer at her for collaborating with the Germans. What did it mean then? What does it mean now? (Grades 7-9)

Magorian, Michelle. *Good Night, Mr. Tom*. New York: Harper, 1982.
When Willie Beech, an abused child of a disturbed single mother, is evacuated from London to the country to escape the Blitz, he is lodged with Mr. Tom. The bitter and reclusive old man learns to love again as he cares for this needy child. A poignant and powerful story. (Grades 7-9)

Matas, Carol. *Lisa's War*. New York: Macmillan, 1987; Scholastic, 1991.
Civilian resistance to the Nazi invasion of Denmark is the subject of this novel for young adults. 7,000 Danish Jews were destined for the concentration camps. Through the individual and collective efforts of people like fourteen-year-old Lisa, her family, and friends, all but 474 escaped safely to neutral Sweden. *Code Name Kris* (Scribner's, 1989) is the sequel, which continues the story of the Danish resistance during World War II. (Grades 8-10)

Mazer, Harry. *The Last Mission*. New York: Delacorte, 1979; Dell, 1981.
Jack Raab is only 15, definitely too young to enlist; but as an American Jew, he feels compelled to try to kill Hitler himself. He uses his older brother's birth certificate and bluffs his way into the Army Air Corps. As one of a crew flying bombing missions over Europe, he sees plenty of action. Then in the last days of the war, his best buddy dies and Jack is shot down behind enemy lines and taken prisoner by the Germans. This novel has the gritty realism of a good war story; Jack swears and sweats convincingly. Details of life in a bomber squadron ring true, as does the awkwardness of Jack's return to civilian life. His growing distaste for the war he has fought so bravely culminates in a touching anti-war speech he gives for his high school class in an assembly called to honor the school's military heroes. (Grades 9-12)

McGraw, Eloise. *The Striped Ships*. New York: McElderry/Macmillan, 1991.
Eleven-year-old Juliana has slipped away from the ladies doing embroidery when she sees the Norman ships coming to invade England. The Saxons are quickly conquered, and her life is never the same again. Later she learns to make peace with the terrors of her experiences when she becomes one of the craft-

speople creating the Bayeux Tapestry, and she is able to insert the Saxon point of view into that history of the Norman conquest. (Grades 7-9)

Miklowitz, Gloria D. *After the Bomb*. New York: Scholastic, 1985.
When a Soviet nuclear bomb is accidentally exploded above the city of Los Angeles, Philip discovers that he has unexpected reserves of strength for coping with the disaster. The author has tried to present the chaos and devastation resulting from a nuclear attack on an urban area realistically. Some readers may feel that it is too optimistic a picture. (Grades 7-10)

————. *Standing Tall, Looking Good*. New York: Delacorte, 1991.
A story about three young people from southern California—a white girl, a wealthy white boy, and an African-American boy—who volunteer to join the army and become adults in the process. The focus is on each person's decision to join and on their experiences in basic training. This is not a distinguished novel, but it is the only one written for young people that presents a picture of contemporary military life. (Grades 8-12)

Moeri, Louise. *The Forty-Third War*. New York: Houghton Mifflin, 1989.
Uno and Lalo are only 12 years old when they are conscripted by the revolutionary forces in an unnamed Central American country. Although they are extremely reluctant recruits, they eventually come to identify with the men and the cause surrounding them. A touching novel about two very young soldiers. (Grades 8-10)

Murray, Michele. *The Crystal Nights*. Clarion, 1973.
Fifteen-year-old Elly has romantic ideas about her beautiful, wealthy cousin Margot, suffering under the beginning of Hitler's persecution of the Jews in Nazi Germany. When Aunt Anna and Margot arrive as refugees and move in with Elly's family, reality intrudes. In a difficult year of mutual adjustments, Elly becomes more aware of the world around her and her place in it. (Grades 7-9)

Myers, Walter Dean. *Fallen Angels*. New York: Scholastic, 1988.
Richie Perry, born and raised in Harlem, had the grades to go to college, but not the money, so he enlists in the army. He expects to play basketball and get enough exposure to get the attention of a pro team. Instead, he is sent to Vietnam. This is the story of Richie and the other eighteen-year-olds, the angel warriors who have been sent to fight a dirty war they barely understand. There are enough gritty, bloody battle scenes to satisfy young men looking for action in their war novels and enough introspection to help them understand their horror. (Grades 8-10)

Naylor, Phyllis Reynolds. *The Dark of the Tunnel*. New York: Atheneum, 1985.
When a small mountain community is asked to mount a civil defense drill as preparation for a possible nuclear attack, it raises issues about the government's motives, the nature of nuclear wars, and the meaning of community. (Grades 8-10)

Nelson, Theresa. *And One for All*. New York: Orchard, 1989.

It is 1967, and the United States is increasingly committed to the war in Vietnam. A younger sister watches her troubled older brother Wing drop out of school and into the Marines while his best friend Sam gets increasingly involved with the anti-war movement. When Wing is killed in the war, Geraldine and her family come to terms with Sam and his motivations. (Grades 7-9)

Noonan, Michael. *McKenzie's Boots*. New York: Orchard, 1987.

This is the story of the life and death of an underage Australian soldier in World War II, an account of wartime heroism told with affection and sincerity. (Grades 8-10)

O'Brien, Robert C. *Z for Zachariah*. New York: Atheneum, 1975; Collier, 1987.

Sixteen-year-old Ann thinks that she is the last person alive in a world that has been destroyed by nuclear radiation until a man walks into her valley wearing a "safe suit." There is much irony in her growing realization that she has more to fear from him than from the toxic world that she inhabits. (Grades 8-10)

Paterson, Katherine. *Of Nightingales That Weep*. Illustrated by Haru Wells. New York: Crowell, 1974.

Set in the feudal world of twelfth century Japan, this story of the war between the Heike and the Genji clans is seen through the eyes of a samurai's daughter. As her clan loses its supremacy in the sweeping and brutal warfare, she gains a more genuine sense of her own identity and duty. (Grades 7-10)

―――. *Rebels of the Heavenly Kingdom*. New York: Dutton, 1983.

Both the glory and the horror of war are presented in this novel about the ill-fated Taiping Rebellion in nineteenth century China. Wang Lee learns to kill for the glory of the Heavenly Kingdom and then learns to feel disgust and shame for the killing. A complex novel about war that also contains some interesting commentary on gender roles. (Grades 7-10)

Paulsen, Gary. *The Cookcamp*. New York: Orchard, 1991.

In 1944, a five-year-old boy sees his mother grow more and more bored. His father is away fighting the war, and his mother is tired of sitting in their apartment, listening to the radio, smoking cigarettes, and waiting. She takes a job in a factory, even though they don't really need the money. Then Casey starts to come around, ". . . and that first night the boy came out of the bedroom in their small apartment and saw his mother with Casey on the couch making sounds he did not understand but did not like . . ." (p. 3). His mother sees the boy watching and sends him off by train to stay with his grandmother in a cookcamp in the northern Minnesota woods, where nine big men are building a road to help the war effort. His grandmother is loving, and the men are kind, treating him like a small but important mascot. When the boy tells her about Casey, the grandmother writes all night for seven nights and mails the letters to her daughter. But one day the boy starts to cry, missing his mother. One of the men says, "It's this damn war. Women out working in the cities. Who ever heard of such a thing?" (p. 101). So the grandmother sends the boy back home. The mother cries when she meets the boy's train, and she looks to the boy just like his grandmother whom he won't see again until he is quite grown up. A haunting, elusive memoir that presents yet another aspect of a child's experience of war. (Grades 7-10)

――――. *The Monument*. New York: Delacorte, 1991.

Mick Strum has been commissioned to create a war memorial monument for a small Kansas town. In the process, a young girl learns that she wants to be an artist, the townspeople learn much about themselves, and the reader learns that art can shape beauty even from the ugliness of war. (Grades 7-10)

――――. *Sentries*. New York: Bradbury, 1986.

The author presents vignettes in the lives of four contemporary young people and three veterans whose war experiences had been particularly traumatic. The young people are all at the moment in their lives when things are coming together and the future seems rich with potential, as the soldiers had been before their lives were changed forever in battle. There is a sense of foreboding which is strengthened by the last chapter which ends with an enormous CLICK. This is a particularly elusive, ambiguous novel, which may or may not be about the end of the world in a nuclear holocaust. (Grades 7-10)

Perez, N.A. *The Slopes of War: A Novel of Gettysburg*. New York: Houghton Mifflin, 1984.

This is a complex novel, with vivid scenes of battle juxtaposed with the thoughts and experiences of soldiers on both sides and ordinary people of the town of Gettysburg. Rebekah Summerhill provides a focus for the reader. A fifteen-year-old girl living in Gettysburg, whose brother fights for the Union and whose cousins fight for the Confederacy in this terrible battle, she learns first-hand the tragic consequences of war. (Grades 8-10)

Peyton, K.M. *The Edge of the Cloud*. Illustrated by Victor G. Ambrus. New York: World, 1969.

――――. *Flambards*. Illustrated by Victor G. Ambrus. New York: World, 1968.

――――. *Flambards in Summer*. Illustrated by Victor G. Ambrus. New York: World, 1969.

The Flambards trilogy provides a rich look at England during World War I, a time of tremendous social change. Christina is an appealing heroine, and the story of her transition from orphan to young bride to widow is well told. The trilogy also provides a fascinating glimpse at the early days of aviation. (Grades 8-12)

Pople, Maureen. *The Other Side of the Family*. New York: Holt, 1986.

Fifteen-year-old Kate is evacuated to her mother's parents in Sydney, Australia. When the Japanese start bombing Sydney, she is sent to her father's mother in the outback. She discovers some remarkable truths about her family and herself in this wry, amusing story. (Grades 7-9)

Poynter, Margaret. *A Time Too Swift*. New York: Atheneum, 1990.
Wartime San Diego is seen through the eyes of a fifteen-year-old girl. At first there is the excitement of a romance with a young marine; later there is the puzzling and harsh treatment of a Japanese-American family and news of death and destruction. (Grades 8-10)

Rinaldi, Ann. *A Ride into Morning: The Story of Tempe Wick*. San Diego: Harcourt Brace Jovanovich, 1991.
This entry in the Great Episodes series attempts to flesh out the legend of Tempe Wick, the New Jersey girl who hid her horse in the house to keep the Pennsylvania army from stealing it. Unfortunately, little is added to our understanding of this legendary event or of the Revolutionary War itself. (Grades 8-10)

————. *Time Enough for Drums*. New York: Holiday House, 1986.
The Revolutionary War is seen through the eyes of fifteen-year-old Jemima Emerson in Trenton, New Jersey. The romantic plot cannot effectively carry the weight of the historical details. (Grades 8-10)

Rostkowski, Margaret I. *After the Dancing Days*. New York: Harper & Row, 1986.
A young adolescent girl confronts her own feelings and asserts her growing sense of self when, against her mother's wishes, she volunteers to work with soldiers who were wounded in the fighting of World War I. The author uses the coming of age theme as a vehicle for presenting a complex, compelling message about how individuals and a society respond to the legacy of war. (Grades 7-9)

Sevela, Ephraim. *We Were Not Like Other People*. Translated from the Russian by Antonina W. Bouis. New York: Harper & Row, 1989.
This is the odyssey of an adolescent boy left alone in Russia at the start of World War II when his father disappears in a Stalinist purge and his mother is apparently killed by a bombing attack. It is an earthy, optimistic story. (Grades 8-10)

Shore, Laura Jan. *The Sacred Moon Tree*. New York: Bradbury, 1986.
Phoebe and her friend Joth set off from Pennsylvania to rescue Joth's brother who is being held in a Confederate prison hospital. The main characters in this picaresque novel are endowed with motivations and attitudes more suited to the 1980s than the 1860s, and there are some offensive descriptions of blacks. A spunky heroine is trapped in an unconvincing historical novel. (Grades 7-9)

Suhl, Yuri. *On the Other Side of the Gate*. New York: Watts, 1975.
Lena and Hershel Bergman are determined to save their baby, David, born secretly inside the Polish ghetto where the Nazis have confined the Jews. This is the story of the elaborate plan which finally results in the baby's safe arrival with a sympathetic Polish family on the other side of the gate. (Grades 8-10)

————. *Uncle Mischa's Partisans*. New York: Four Winds Press, 1973.
Twelve-year-old Motele has sought out the Jewish partisans who hide out in the forests of the Ukraine. Now he longs to work actively to avenge his family's death by Nazi soldiers. Eventually, he has the opportunity to infiltrate a German

stronghold and play an important role in the bombing of the Nazi headquarters there. (Grades 7-9)

Sutcliff, Rosemary. *The Capricorn Bracelet*. Illustrated by Richard Cuffari. New York: Walck, 1973.

The history of Roman Britain is seen through episodes in the lives of six members of a family of soldiers. This is a fascinating look at an interesting period and a brilliant approach to military history. (Grades 8-10)

————. *The Shining Company*. New York: Farrar Straus Giroux, 1990.

King Mynyddog raises an army of 300 young men and sends them to fight against the invading Saxons. Supported by their shieldbearers, the Companions form a shining company and fight valiantly in the face of overwhelming odds but are ultimately slaughtered. Two men survive, only to learn that they had been sent on a suicide mission to fight a battle the king knew they could not win. Young readers who are able to handle the unfamiliar names and events and Sutcliff's dense, descriptive prose will share the disillusionment and despair of the betrayed warriors. (Grades 8-10)

————. *Song for a Dark Queen*. New York: Crowell, 1979.

Here is the bloody, passionate story of the doomed warrior queen Boadicea who led her British tribes in a futile revolt against Roman rule in 62 A.D. (Grades 8-12)

————. *Warrior Scarlet*. Illustrated by Charles Keeping. New York: Walck, 1958.

This is not a story about war, but rather a story about the making of a warrior in Bronze Age Britain. The hero of the novel is a boy with a crippled arm who perseveres and finally proves himself worthy to be a warrior of his tribe. (Grades 8-10)

Taylor, Mildred D. *The Road to Memphis*. New York: Dial, 1990.

In 1941, the United States is concerned with the war in Europe. For Cassie Logan and the other young African-Americans in rural Mississippi, racism is a more immediate concern. The decisions that these young black men make about whether or not to enlist as soldiers have a different calculus than the decisions of their white counterparts. (Grades 8-12)

Tolan, Stephanie S. *Pride of the Peacock*. New York: Scribner's, 1986.

After reading about the threat of nuclear destruction in Jonathan Schell's *Fate of the Earth*, thirteen-year-old Whitney is profoundly depressed. An old school friend and a new adult friend who is mourning the death of her husband help her to find a way to live with hope. Whitney is a believable adolescent whose struggle to understand and cope with the nuclear threat is portrayed with understated sensitivity. (Grades 7-10)

Tunis, John R. *His Enemy, His Friend*. New York: Morrow, 1967.

In 1944, in occupied France, six hostages are killed by the Germans in retaliation for the death of a German soldier. Twenty years later, the son of one of the hostages and the German officer in charge of the village where the incident occurred face each other on the soccer field in a European championship match. (Grades 7-10)

Walsh, Jill Paton. *Fireweed*. New York: Farrar, Straus & Giroux, 1969.
This novel is about survival, young love, and the British class system. Set in London during the Blitz, it tells the story of a teenage boy and girl on their own in a time of great danger. Their survival is heroic; their love story is tender and bittersweet. A rewarding literary experience. (Grades 7-9)

Westall, Robert. *Echoes of War*. New York: Farrar, Straus and Giroux, 1991.
Five sophisticated, haunting stories about the impact of war on young people. (Grades 8-10)

————. *The Machine Gunners*. New York: Greenwillow, 1976.
It is 1941 in Garmouth, a British village that has been heavily bombed in the Blitz. Chas McGill, a young teenager, happens on a German plane that has been shot down in a wood near town. The pilot is dead, but his machine gun is intact. Chas and his friends concoct a scheme to mount the machine gun and join in a direct attack on the German bombers. This novel was awarded England's Carnegie Medal for distinction in children's literature in 1976, and much of its distinction lies in the subtlety of its portrayal of human responses to war. The children who are at the center of this book at first find the war an irritant, then a source of novelty as they collect shrapnel, and finally an opportunity for deeds of valor as they embark on the grand adventure with their own machine gun. Their hatred of the Germans is tempered by their growing intimacy with a real German who stumbles on their hidden gun emplacement and becomes their prisoner—and colleague—for a time. One sees both the plucky heroism that has become part of the mythology of the British civilian experience of World War II and the terrifying consequences of human error when weapons of destruction are involved. The ambiguity is not brought into artificially sharp focus for the young readers who will identify with both the dreams of heroism and the natural fears of the children who sometimes seem as much at war with the authorities in their own village as they do with the German enemy. At one point, Chas ponders whether to tell his father about the machine gun: "But could any grownup keep you safe now? They couldn't stop the German bombers . . . . He looked at his father, and saw a weary, helpless middle-aged man. Dad wasn't any kind of God any more. Chas screwed himself up to life" (p. 93). In the sequel, *Fathom Five* (Greenwillow, 1980), Chas and his friends try to catch a spy who is sabotaging shipments of materiel from the local harbor. (Grades 7-10)

White, Robb. *The Frogmen*. New York: Doubleday, 1973.
This novel is representative of other World War II adventure stories written by White. Here the plot revolves around the efforts of four oddly assorted Navy personnel to discover the secrets of the mined channel to a key Japanese atoll and to get the word back to American troops. There is little irony or ambiguity here, just action and suspense. (Grades 7-10)

Nonfiction

Abels, Chana Byers. *The Children We Remember*. New York: Greenwillow, 1986.

> Haunting, poignant, terrifying pictures of children who died during the Holocaust—and a few who survived—tell a story that will be difficult for children to process without wise adults to help interpret, explain, reassure, and console. (Grades 4+)

Adler, David A. *The Number on My Grandfather's Arm*. New York: UAHC Press, 1987.

> A simple first person text and black-and-white photos tell the story of a little girl's grandfather who listens when she talks to him, mends her torn clothes, tells her stories about when he was young in a small village in Eastern Europe, and always wears shirts with long sleeves. One night he rolls up his sleeves to help with the dishes, and she sees the number tattooed on his arm. "It's time you told her," says the little girl's mother, and Grandpa does tell her about how Hitler's Nazis tried to kill all the Jews in Europe, and how lucky he was to survive. Afterwards, the girl puts her hand on her grandpa's and tells him, "You shouldn't be ashamed to let people see your number. You didn't do anything wrong. It's the Nazis who should be ashamed." (Grades Kindergarten-2)

Ashabranner, Brent. *Always to Remember: The Story of the Vietnam Veterans Memorial*. Illustrated by Jennifer Ashabranner. New York: Dodd, Mead, 1988.

> The eloquent photos focus on the memorial itself and the visitors who come there. The text deals with the people responsible for creating the memorial and the war that inspired it. (Grades 5-8)

————. *A Grateful Nation: The Story of Arlington National Cemetery*. Photographs by Jennifer Ashabranner. New York: Putnam, 1990.

> In addition to telling the history of the national burial ground where more than 200,000 war veterans and their dependents are interred, the straightforward text and photos give information about the Tomb of the Unknown Soldier, military burials, and some of the famous people whose graves are here. (Grades 5-8)

Ashabranner, Brent, and Melissa Ashabranner. *Into a Strange Land: Unaccompanied Refugee Youth in America*. New York: Dodd, Mead, 1987.

> The authors present stories and photos of young people who have come to the United States as refugees from wars and political unrest from all parts of the world, but primarily from Southeast Asia. (Grades 6-9)

Atkinson, Linda. *In Kindling Flame: The Story of Hannah Senesh, 1921-1944*. New York: Lothrop, Lee & Shepard, 1985.

> This handsomely produced book tells the story of a young Hungarian Jew who started a new life in Palestine but returned to Hungary in 1944 as part of a team of resistance fighters determined to save the lives of the Jews who remained there. She was caught and executed and is remembered today as a heroic martyr who defended her people and her beliefs. (Grades 7-10)

Auerbacher, Inge. *I Am a Star: Child of the Holocaust.* Illustrated by Israel Birnbaum. New York: Prentice-Hall, 1986.

> This is a first-hand account by one of the very few children to survive the Nazi concentration camp of Terezin. It has an immediacy and authenticity lacking in many other stories of the Holocaust. On the book jacket is a statement from Bruno Bettelheim: "Without stressing the horrors she lived through, the author tells her story in a way that should permit young people to grasp what the holocaust was like. She does so without making them feel guilty or giving them nightmares, shortcomings of so many other reports on the holocaust." (Grades 5-7)

Bernbaum, Israel. *My Brother's Keeper: The Holocaust Through the Eyes of an Artist.* New York: Putnam's, 1985.

> The author and artist responsible for this book escaped from Warsaw just before the ghetto walls were erected. When he grew up, he created a series of five paintings about the Warsaw Ghetto. This book contains the paintings and the author's commentary about them, as well as maps and photos of Warsaw. It is an intensely personal interpretation. (Grades 5-8)

Bernheim, Mark. *Father of the Orphans: The Story of Januscz Korczak.* New York: Dutton, 1989.

> The author attempts to make the life of this complex man accessible to young readers. While his motivations remain shadowy, the man's commitment to children and his poignant accompaniment of the Jewish orphans to their death in Treblinka are vividly portrayed. (Grades 7-10)

Black, Sheila. *Sitting Bull and the Battle of the Little Bighorn.* Englewood Cliffs, NJ: Silver Burdett, 1989.

> This biography portrays Sitting Bull as a holy man and religious leader as well as a warrior. (Grades 5-8)

Bratman, Fred. *War in the Persian Gulf.* Brookfield, CT: Millbrook, 1991.

> While this book claims to be an objective account of the stories behind the headlines during the Persian Gulf War, it is entirely uncritical. There is no mention of any objection to the war in the United States or of any negative consequences. However, some of the tables and sidebars in the book contain useful information, and a photo of a female soldier with names for all of her gear makes the point that women played an active part in this military action. (Grades 4-6)

Byam, Michele. *Arms and Armor.* New York: Knopf, 1988.

> This addition to the Eyewitness Books series contains enough photographs and drawings of hand weapons such as boomerangs, swords, crossbows, maces, pistols, rifles, muskets, and tomahawks to satisfy the most curious child. The coverage is global and dates from prehistoric times to the nineteenth century. (Grades 3-6)

Chaikin, Miriam. *Light Another Candle: The Story and Meaning of Hanukkah*. Illustrated by Demi. New York: Clarion, 1981.

This book contains much lore about the Jewish holiday of Hanukkah, including its beginning with the victory of the Jewish resistance fighters over the forces of the Greek ruler Antiochus 2000 years ago. (Grades 3-6)

Chang, Ina. *A Separate Battle: Women and the Civil War*. New York: Lodestar/Dutton, 1991.

A readable text, along with well-chosen historical documents and photos, highlights the roles that women played in the Civil War. Some of these women are well known, such as Clara Barton, Harriet Tubman, and Louisa Alcott. Others that will be less familiar to young readers include the Confederate spy, Belle Boyd, and Sarah Edmonds and Loreta Velasquez, who disguised themselves as men in order to serve as soldiers. (Grades 5-9)

Coolidge, Olivia. *The Trojan War*. Illustrated by Edouard Sandoz. New York: Houghton Mifflin, 1952.

Drawing from the *Iliad*, the *Odyssey*, and Greek mythology, the author presents a cohesive account of the Trojan War. Warfare is the setting here for grand deeds of courage and caprice, heroism and foolishness, romance and revenge. (Grades 7-9)

Cowan, Lore. *Children of the Resistance*. New York: Meredith, 1969.

These accounts of children or young teenagers who actively resisted the Nazi regime include Yugoslavian partisans who took arms against the German invaders, a deaf and dumb French boy who helped find and hide Allied pilots who were shot down, and a group of Dutch children who actively sabotaged Nazi efforts to supply their troops with food. While the author claims the stories are true, the narratives themselves are heavily fictionalized. (Grades 6-9)

Cox, Clinton. *Undying Glory: The Story of the Massachusetts 54th Regiment*. New York: Scholastic, 1991.

In addition to the history of the all-black "Glory" regiment, Cox presents background materials about the Civil War that are not readily available in other books. We learn here, for example, about the draft riots in New York City, in which mobs of white men turned their fury about being drafted to fight slavery against black people living in the city, eventually burning the Colored Orphan Asylum on Fifth Avenue. (Grades 5-8)

Cummings, Richard. *Make Your Own Model Forts and Castles*. New York: David McKay, 1977.

Detailed instructions are given for making seven models, each based on an actual fortification or battlefield. This is an excellent companion to James Giblin's *Walls: Defenses Throughout History* and many of the novels in this bibliography. (Grades 4+)

Davis, Burke. *Black Heroes of the American Revolution*. San Diego: Harcourt Brace Jovanovich, 1976.

Prints and portraits from the period enhance this gathering of information about the unsung African-Americans who helped to win American independence, often without achieving their own. (Grades 4-6)

Demi. *Chingis Khan*. New York: Holt, 1991.

A brilliantly illustrated, easy-to-read biography of the great thirteenth century Mongolian warrior and leader. (Grades 2-4)

Donnelly, Judy. *A Wall of Names: The Story of the Vietnam Veterans Memorial*. New York: Random, 1991.

An effective account of the Vietnam Veterans Memorial and the war that it represents. The easy-to-read text and well-selected photos will help the youngest readers to understand this important event in the recent American past. (Grades 2-4)

Everston, Jonathan. *Colin Powell*. New York: Bantam, 1991.

Colin Powell is the first African-American to head the Joint Chiefs of Staff. He came to the attention of the American people during the 1989 military action in Panama in which General Noriega was captured. The War in the Persian Gulf added to his fame. This book contains information about those military campaigns as well as biographical information about Powell. (Grades 4-6)

Finkelstein, Norman H. *Remember Not to Forget: A Memory of the Holocaust*. Illustrated by Lois and Lars Hokanson. New York: Watts, 1985.

A very brief text, illustrated with bold woodcuts, presents the Holocaust in the context of Jewish history. It closes with a description of the mission of Yad Vashem in Israel and the observance of Yom Hashoa, Holocaust Remembrance Day. (Grades 2-4)

Fisher, Leonard Everett. *Cyclops*. New York: Holiday House, 1991.

Returning from the Trojan War, Odysseus and his men are punished by the gods for desecrating Princess Cassandra's temple in Troy. The gods send a fierce storm, driving the ship off course and forcing a landing on an unknown island. There the Greeks encounter the dreadful one-eyed giant, the Cyclops. He keeps them captive in his well-stocked cave, eating them one by one. How the Greeks finally escape by hiding under the bellies of the blinded giant's sheep is a classic tale of military trickery, presented here in simple words and effective illustrations. (Grades 3-5)

Foreman, Michael. *War Boy: A Country Childhood*. New York: Arcade/Little, Brown, 1989.

This profusely illustrated memoir of a boyhood on the Suffolk coast of England during World War II is full of the everyday details that children will appreciate. Foreman draws the exact trajectory of the incendiary bomb that came through the roof over his bed and bounced over his mother's bed, hitting a mirror, before exploding up the chimney. There is inevitably a nostalgic air about the author's remembrances of a time when he was, after all, very happy. (Grades 4+)

Frank, Anne. *Anne Frank: The Diary of a Young Girl.* New York: Simon & Schuster, 1952.

> The continuing appeal of this book with American adolescents is probably based on their identification with Anne, a teenager so much like themselves in her interests and feelings, whose circumstances and ultimate fate are still so different and tragic. That identification—and her matter-of-fact approach to her life in hiding—makes it possible for young readers to put themselves in the otherwise unimaginable horror of her position. (Grades 6+)

Freedman, Russell. *Lincoln: A Photobiography.* New York: Clarion, 1987.

> This biography of Abraham Lincoln deals extensively with the important role he played in the Civil War. One of the rare nonfiction books to be awarded the Newbery medal for distinction in children's literature, this is an excellent introduction to Lincoln and his times. (Grades 5-8)

Friedman, Ina R. *Escape or Die: True Stories of Young People Who Survived the Holocaust.* Reading, MA: Addison-Wesley, 1982.

> This well-chosen collection of survival stories portrays the diversity of escape routes that carried Jews from Nazi Europe to new lives in other parts of the world. (Grades 5-8)

―――. *The Other Victims: First-Person Stories of Non-Jews Persecuted by the Nazis.* Boston: Houghton Mifflin, 1990.

> The author provides historical background as well as first-person retellings of the experiences of Gypsies, homosexuals, dissenters, the physically handicapped, and others who were persecuted by the Nazis. In addition to the six million Jews who died during the Holocaust, there were five million "other victims." (Grades 6-9)

Fritz, Jean. *And Then What Happened, Paul Revere?* Illustrated by Margot Tomes. New York: Coward, McCann, & Geogehagan, 1973.

> This engaging little book tells young readers about the life and times of Paul Revere, and especially what happened on his famous midnight ride to Lexington in 1775. (Grades 2-4)

―――. *Stonewall.* Illustrated by Stephen Gammell. New York: Putnam's, 1979.

> A readable biography of the eccentric Civil War general who held himself erect to avoid displacing his alimentary canal and carried his preferred diet of dry bread and lean meat with him in a bag when invited out to dinner. Some historians might think that Fritz has downplayed his ferociousness in battle. (Grades 5-8)

―――. *Traitor: The Case of Benedict Arnold.* New York: Putnam's, 1981; Puffin, 1989.

> The author brings much historical detail to this life of the complex man whose name has become synonymous with treason for his attempt to betray West Point to the British, yet the reader is still left to wonder about his motivations. Was he driven by greed, as his enemies asserted, or by his own convictions, as he declared in his own defense? (Grades 7-9)

Gates, Doris. *Athena, the Warrior Goddess*. Illustrated by Don Bolognese. New York: Puffin, 1972; Puffin, 1982.

> Athena was the Greek goddess of wisdom, as well as the goddess of war. This selection of myths features Athena in both roles and includes the stories of Perseus and Medusa, Pegasus, Jason and the Argonauts, and Arachne. (Grades 4-6)

Giblin, James Cross. *Walls: Defenses Throughout History*. Boston: Little, Brown, 1984.

> The author presents a history of fortifications, from a wall made of mammoth bones in the Ice Age to the trenches of the Maginot Line in World War II. Illustrated with photos and line drawings, this should both satisfy and pique the curiosity of many children. (Grades 4-6)

Goble, Paul, and Dorothy Goble. *Red Hawk's Account of Custer's Last Battle: The Battle of the Little Bighorn, 25 June 1876*. New York: Pantheon, 1969.

> An account of the Battle of the Little Bighorn from the point of view of a fifteen-year-old Oglala Sioux warrior. Based on many Indian retellings of the battle, the first-person narrative is poetic and immediate. The striking color illustrations were inspired by Plains Indians paintings from the period 1860-1890. (Grades 4-6)

Hamanaka, Sheila. *The Journey: Japanese Americans, Racism, and Renewal*. New York: Orchard, 1990.

> The artist has added words to create a narrative accompaniment to her five-panel mural documenting the history of the Japanese in the United States. The focal point of the mural and the book is the experience of Japanese Americans during World War II. This book is a stunning graphic achievement and a powerful learning experience. (Grades 4-8)

Hamilton, Leni. *Clara Barton*. New York: Chelsea House, 1988.

> This is a well-written, informative biography of the woman who went on from her work as a battlefront nurse during the Civil War to head a nationwide search for missing soldiers after the war. When this task was accomplished, she founded the American Red Cross and succeeded in expanding the mission of the International Red Cross to include disaster relief as well as care for the sick and wounded during war. At age 77, she served as a nurse on the battlefields of Cuba during the Spanish-American War. (Grades 5-9)

Hautzig, Esther. *The Endless Steppe: Growing Up in Siberia*. New York: Crowell, 1968.

> When the Russians occupied northeastern Poland at the beginning of World War II, they arrested the Rudomin family as capitalist "enemies of the state." This is the story of their exile in Siberia, seen through the eyes of Esther, the daughter of the family. The hardships they endure are a wrenching change from their former privileged status, but they survive. Esther actually regrets leaving her friends and the life she knows in the village on the frozen plain when the war is over and the family is reunited in Poland. (Grades 5-8)

Hoobler, Dorothy, and Thomas Hoobler. *The Trenches: Fighting on the Western Front in World War I*. New York: Putnam's, 1978.

> A readable text and well-chosen photos present the rationale, the everyday reality, and the consequences of the trench warfare of World War I. This effectively debunks any romanticized notion of combat. (Grades 5-9)

———. *Vietnam, Why We Fought: An Illustrated History*. New York: Knopf, 1990.

> This is similar in coverage and approach to Margot Mabie's *Vietnam There and Here,* discussed below. The pictorial format is particularly effective here. (Grades 5-8)

Houston, Jeanne Wakatsuki, and James D. Houston. *Farewell to Manzanar*. Boston: Houghton Mifflin, 1973.

> Jeanne was seven years old when her family was taken to the internment camp at Manzanar and eleven when they left, after the bombing of Hiroshima and Nagasaki. The remembered details create an intimate picture of the life behind barbed wire that was uncannily like that of any other American town. (Grades 6+)

Hurwitz, Johanna. *Anne Frank: Life in Hiding*. Illustrated by Vera Rosenberry. Philadelphia: Jewish Publication Society, 1988.

> This brief, well-written biography of Anne Frank could serve as an introduction or as a useful supplement to the diary itself. (Grades 4-6)

Huynh, Quang Nhuong. *The Land I Lost: Adventures of a Boy in Vietnam*. Illustrated by Vo-Dinh Mai. New York: Harper & Row, 1982.

> The author tells stories of his boyhood in the central highlands of Vietnam. Most of the stories are about the animals, both helpful and dangerous, that were a part of everyday life. He remembers encounters with the dreaded horse snake, 200-pound catfish, pythons, and wild hogs. There are several stories about Tank, the beloved family water buffalo who had the rare and desirable qualities of being a good fighter and a hard worker. The last chapter is called "Sorrow." The boy was in the fields with the herd of water buffaloes when fighting broke out in the hamlet between the French forces and Ho Chi Minh's resistance soldiers. Tank is shot and dies. "We buried Tank in the graveyard where we buried all the dead of our family, and every Lunar New Year my father burned incense in front of all the tombs, including Tank's" (p. 115). (Grades 4-6)

Jakes, John. *Susanna of the Alamo: A True Story*. Illustrated by Paul Bacon. San Diego: Harcourt Brace Jovanovich, 1985.

> The author and illustrator of this book present the story of the Alamo as a stirring tale of massacre and revenge. There is little here for the pacifist to endorse, but some readers may be stirred by the book's accounts of valor and heroism. This is vivid historical writing by the author of such adult best-sellers as *North and South,* and an example of effective book design as well. (Grades 4-6)

Katz, William Loren, and Marc Crawford. *The Lincoln Brigade: A Picture History*. New York: Atheneum, 1989.

> A stirring documentary account of the 2800 American volunteers who formed the Abraham Lincoln Brigade in 1936, fighting for the republic in the Spanish Civil War and becoming the first integrated American army. (Grades 6-9)

Kennaley, Lucinda Hedrick. *Only Soldiers Go to War*. Illustrated by Charmaine Curtis. Springfield, MO: Thoth, 1991.

> This hastily published book was intended to explain the Persian Gulf War and justify American involvement in it. It is simplistic, reassuring, patriotic, and appropriate for very young children. (Grades Kindergarten-2)

Kent, Zachary. *The Story of the Rough Riders*. Chicago: Children's Press, 1991.

> The photographs and drawings add considerably to this uncritical account of the volunteers who fought with Teddy Roosevelt in Cuba during the Spanish-American War. (Grades 4-6)

Kherdian, David. *The Road from Home: The Story of an Armenian Girl*. New York: Greenwillow, 1979.

> The author presents his mother's history in the first person, as if she were telling the story. This is another account of refugees fleeing from wartime atrocities, in this case the Turkish effort during World War I to exterminate the Armenians living within Turkish borders. Veron Dumehjian is an appealing spokesperson—clear-eyed, somewhat naive, optimistic, not embittered by the horrors around her. (Grades 5-8)

Koen, Ilse. *Mischling, Second Degree: My Childhood in Nazi Germany*. New York: Greenwillow, 1977; Puffin, 1990.

> The author tells of her girlhood in Germany, a time in which her parents encouraged her to participate actively in the Hitler Youth in spite of their opposition to the Nazi regime. Only when the war is over does she learn that her paternal grandmother was a Jew and that her parents were protecting her from possible death at the hands of the Nazis. (Grades 6-8)

Kuskin, Karla. *Jerusalem, Shining Still*. Illustrated by David Frampton. New York: Harper, 1987.

> A brief lyrical text and stunning woodcuts present the history of Jerusalem as a series of wars, one conquest after another for more than 4000 years. (Grades 4-6)

Lifton, Betty Jean. *Return to Hiroshima*. Photographs by Eikoh Hosoe. New York: Atheneum, 1970.

> This commemorates the twenty-fifth anniversary of the bombing of Hiroshima. A poetic text and eloquent black-and-white photos evoke the significance of that event for its survivors and for the rest of humanity. (Grades 6+)

Lifton, Betty Jean, and Thomas C. Fox. *Children of Vietnam*. New York: Atheneum, 1972.

> Written while the Vietnam War was still unresolved, this collection of vignettes portrays children from several segments of Vietnamese society—refugees, war

orphans, street children, Amerasians, privileged youth, urban children, and peasants. Nobody reading this could doubt the effects of that war, or any war, on children. (Grades 5-9)

Mabie, Margot C.J. *Vietnam There and Here*. New York: Holt, Rinehart and Winston, 1985.

Written on the tenth anniversary of the end of the war in Vietnam, this is an even-handed explanation of what happened in both Vietnam and the United States during that confrontation. This book was intended for readers who are too young to have any first-hand knowledge of the event, and it includes phonetic guides for pronouncing Vietnamese names and a useful glossary. (Grades 5-8)

Mansfield, Sue, and Mary Bowen Hall. *Some Reasons for War: How Families, Myths and Warfare Are Connected*. New York: Crowell, 1988.

A historian and an educator trace the psychological reasons why people go to war. *Why Are There Wars? Powerful Ideas for Teaching Writing Skills* by Mary Bowen Hall and Sue Mansfield (listed in the bibliography in the "Parenting, Teaching, Guiding" section) presents curriculum units based on the ideas in this book. (Grades 6+)

Marrin, Albert. *Hitler*. New York: Viking, 1987.

While some detail about Hitler's life is provided, this is primarily the story of his policies, his regime, and his war. (Grades 5-9)

————. *The Spanish-American War*. New York: Atheneum, 1991.

The author, a professor of history at Yeshiva University in New York, presents a balanced, well-written account of the war that gave the American people yellow journalism, Teddy Roosevelt's Rough Riders, and the beginning of a long entanglement with the Philippines. (Grades 5-9)

————. *War Clouds in the West: Indians and Cavalrymen, 1860-1890*. New York: Atheneum, 1984.

This account of 30 particularly bloody years in the long war that the United States government waged against the Indian nations depicts horrors perpetrated by each side. It is clear, however, that the author is sympathetic to the Native Americans who were fighting for a way of life and for land that had always been theirs. (Grades 5-9)

Maruki, Toshi. *Hiroshima No Pika*. New York: Lothrop, 1980.

This is the story of the bombing of Hiroshima as it affected a representative family with a seven-year-old daughter. The text is brief and clear, and the visual images are strong. Most young children will need help interpreting this powerful book. (Grades 4-6)

McGovern, Ann. *The Secret Soldier: The Story of Deborah Sampson*. Illustrated by Ann Grifalconi. New York: Four Winds, 1975.

An appealing biography of the woman who disguised herself as a man and served in the Continental Army for a year and a half. (Grades 2-4)

Meltzer, Milton. *Bound for the Rio Grande: The Mexican Struggle, 1845-1850.* New York: Knopf, 1974.

Using original source materials such as letters, diaries, speeches, and songs, Meltzer traces the history and results of the first American offensive war, fought under the banner of Manifest Destiny. (Grades 7-10)

————. *Hunted Like a Wolf: The Story of the Seminole War.* New York: Farrar, Straus & Giroux, 1972.

The opening chapter outlines the history and policies that led to the Seminole War, the longest and costliest of the Indian wars. Relying on primary sources and sound historical accounts, Meltzer presents an uncompromising account of an unjust war waged by the government of the United States against its own people in the years from 1835 to 1842. (Grades 7+)

————. *Never to Forget: The Jews of the Holocaust.* New York: Harper & Row, 1976; HarperTrophy, 1991.

A thorough, dispassionate treatment of the background, events, and consequences of the Holocaust. The discussion of Jewish resistance is particularly useful. (Grades 7+)

————. *Rescue: The Story of How Gentiles Saved Jews in the Holocaust.* New York: Harper & Row, 1988.

The author presents this as a companion to *Never to Forget*, which focused on the victims of the Holocaust. In the introduction, he regrets that the rescuers were so few but makes the point that their actions were important, helping us see that we have choices and need not give in to evil. Young readers will find in this book the stories of individuals, such as Raoul Wallenberg, and of whole nations, such as Denmark. (Grades 7+)

Miller, Robert. *The Buffalo Soldiers.* Illustrated by Richard Leonard. Englewood Cliffs, NJ: Silver Burdett 1991.

In this second volume of *Reflections of a Black Cowboy*, the narrator, called Old Cowboy, tells his dog Sundance stories of the Buffalo Soldiers, the African-Americans who served in the Ninth and Tenth cavalries. Although the dialogue and dialect are sometimes a little forced, the stories are worth hearing—about the first black soldier to win the Medal of Honor, the first to graduate from West Point, and the troops who won the day at the Battle of San Juan Hill during the Spanish-American War. The ironies involved in black men fighting Indians and in fighting for a country that failed to give them equal rights are mentioned but not emphasized. (Grades 5-7)

Morimoto, Junko. *My Hiroshima.* New York: Viking, 1990.

The author/illustrator shares her childhood memories of the bombing of Hiroshima. The words are simple, and the pictures are childlike, making this an appropriate book for parents who want to help younger children understand the effects of nuclear warfare. The images are too graphic, however, for most young children to process without sensitive adult intervention. (Grades 3-5)

Morris, Ann. *When Will the Fighting Stop? A Child's View of Jerusalem.* Photographs by Lilly Rivlin. New York: Atheneum, 1990.

A young Jewish boy wanders through the city of Jerusalem, where he lives. He sees an Arab washing himself before he prays, Christian pilgrims, Jews praying at the Wailing Wall, and an Israeli soldier with a gun. He sees the little Arab girl whose father will no longer let him play with her. He is angry because he is not welcome in some parts of the city, and he wonders when peace will come to his city. Unfortunately, this photo essay does little to inform about the long history of competing interests that prevent peace from coming, but it could lead to a discussion about the complex issues surrounding Middle East peace prospects. (Grades 3-5)

Murphy, Jim. *The Boys' War: Confederate and Union Soldiers Talk About the Civil War.* New York: Clarion, 1990.

The author uses letters, diaries, and memoirs to tell the story of the Civil War as experienced by the estimated 250,000 to 420,000 boys under the age of sixteen who fought on both sides. From the drummer boys and telegraph operators to the tall fourteen-year-olds who lied about their age, they joined up with youthful dreams of glory and experienced the same battle horrors as men twice their age. Photographs heighten the impact of their stories—twelve-year-old Johnny Clem after the Battle of Shiloh, William Black who was twelve when he was wounded by a shell, a fourteen-year-old Confederate soldier lying dead at Fort Mahone. This is history at its most compelling. (Grades 5-9)

"My Desert Storm" Workbook: First Aid for Feelings. New York: Workman, 1991.

Prepared by the National Childhood Grief Institute and issued while Operation Desert Storm was still being fought, this workbook was designed to help children deal with the feelings of fear and anxiety caused by the war. It is full of blank pages on which the child is encouraged to write down what war means to him or her, to draw expressions on faces that show how the child feels about the war, etc. An introductory message to adults gives advice on how to use the book to help children cope with feelings of vulnerability that result from exposure to war. (Grades 2-5)

Neimark, Anne E. *Che! Latin America's Guerilla Leader.* New York: Lippincott, 1989.

A thoughtful, objective biography that deals with Che Guevara's political motivations as well as his guerilla tactics and attempts to explain his enduring appeal as a symbolic revolutionary leader. (Grades 5-8)

Patent, Gregory. *Shanghai Passage.* Illustrated by Ted Lewin. New York: Clarion, 1990.

The author recalls his childhood as the son of a Russian father and an Iraqi mother in Shanghai during World War II and its chaotic aftermath. There is a glow of nostalgia here that is common to many memoirs of wartime childhoods when the battles and deprivations remained somewhat remote. (Grades 4-6)

Pringle, Laurence. *Nuclear War: From Hiroshima to Nuclear Winter.* Hillside, NJ: Enslow, 1985.

The former editor of *Nature and Science* magazine has written an understandable, objective account of the history of nuclear warfare from World War II to the mid-1980s. Current easing of tensions between the United States and the former Soviet republics is not reflected. (Grades 5-9)

Rabinowitz, Richard. *What Is War? What Is Peace? 50 Questions and Answers for Kids.* New York: Avon, 1991.

Using the Persian Gulf War as a springboard, the author goes on to answer such questions as "Why did we get involved with Kuwait?" "How do military leaders decide what to do in a war?" "How do you get to be a soldier?" "What happens when a soldier gets sick or hurt?" "Can you be against the war but still be patriotic?" "What happens to a kid if his or her parents are soldiers at war?" This is one of the more even-handed and objective books to emerge about the Persian Gulf War, although it doesn't address the issue of civilian casualties in either a general or specific context. (Grades 4-6)

Ray, Delia. *Behind the Blue and Gray: The Soldier's Life in the Civil War.* New York: Lodestar/Dutton, 1991.

This is another excellent addition to the Young Readers' History of the Civil War series. Using many first-person accounts, historical documents, and photos from the period, the author brings to life the everyday experiences of soldiers on both sides of the Civil War. (Grades 5-9)

———. *A Nation Torn: The Story of How the Civil War Began.* New York: Lodestar/Dutton, 1990.

This well-researched and well-written account of the events leading up to the Civil War would be excellent background material for many of the novels about that period, particularly those set in the border states of Kansas and Missouri. (Grades 5-9)

Reit, Seymour. *Behind Rebel Lines: The Incredible Story of Emma Edmonds, Civil War Spy.* San Diego: Harcourt Brace Jovanovich, 1988.

Emma Edmonds was a truly astonishing heroine of the Civil War. Disguising herself as a man, she enlisted in the Union Army. Not satisfied with that feat, she donned another array of disguises, including that of a slave, and served as a spy behind the Confederate lines. This lively biography is flawed by an over-reliance on contrived dialogue, but it should appeal to young readers looking for stories about strong women. (Grades 4-6)

Rogasky, Barbara. *Smoke and Ashes: The Story of the Holocaust.* New York: Holiday House, 1988.

This is a remarkable book, direct and honest, caring and compassionate. The author sets the tone from the first page: "This book was not written to give you nightmares." She goes on to say: "Reading about it is not easy. The figures are large and there are many of them. The details are unpleasant and cruel, perhaps even painful to read. But the story cannot be made pretty, like a tale told to little children. There is no happy ending" (p.5). Forewarned, children can go on to read in forceful, simple prose, illustrated with photos from the period, about the nightmare that came true. Hopefully, there will be informed and sensitive adults to guide children after they have read the book. (Grades 5-8)

Salzman, Marian, and Ann O'Reilly. *War and Peace in the Persian Gulf: What Teenagers Want to Know*. Princeton: NJ: Petersen's Guides, 1991.

An unusual and admirable feature of this book is the inclusion of quotes from teenagers throughout the country, expressing their questions, concerns, and ideas about the Persian Gulf War. Since the book was rushed to publication while interest in the war was high, it doesn't deal with the consequences of the war but is quite wide-ranging in its coverage nonetheless, including chapters on the effects of the war on the environment and the controversy about media coverage. A particularly useful feature is a detailed timeline of war events. (Grades 7+)

Sender, Ruth Minsky. *The Cage*. New York: Macmillan, 1986.

In this compelling autobiography by a Holocaust survivor, the reader experiences the rage, despair, determination, and helplessness the author felt as a prisoner of the Nazis in the Lodz Ghetto and then in Auschwitz. (Grades 6-9)

Shorto, Russell. *Geronimo and the Struggle for Apache Freedom*. Illustrated by L.L. Cundiff. Englewood Cliffs, NJ: Silver Burdett, 1989.

A clearly written biography of Goyathlay, the Bedonkohe Apache boy who grew up to be the warrior Geronimo. The author is careful to present the Native American perspective on the bloody wars between the Apaches and the U.S. soldiers. (Grades 5-8)

Shura, Mary Francis. *Gentle Annie: The True Story of a Civil War Nurse*. New York: Scholastic, 1991.

While based on facts, this is a considerably fictionalized biography of one woman who served as a volunteer nurse for the Union during the Civil War. Another heroine of the Civil War, Sarah Emma Edmonds, makes a cameo appearance in her male disguise as Frank Thompson, an intrepid spy for the North. (Grades 5-8)

Siegal, Aranka. *Upon the Head of the Goat: A Childhood in Hungary, 1939-1944*. New York: Farrar Straus Giroux, 1981.

The author remembers her childhood as part of a happy middle-class Jewish family in Beregszasz, Hungary. Things change forever when the Germans take over her country. It begins with curfews and the identifying Star of David. Then the Jews are confined to a ghetto and finally removed to Auschwitz. Remarkably, the author and two sisters survive, although the rest of the family perishes in the Holocaust. The sequel, *Grace in the Wilderness: After the Liberation, 1945-1948* (Farrar Straus Giroux, 1985) follows the author and one sister in the critical years after the war, when they are taken to Sweden and try to reconstruct normal lives out of abnormal circumstances. Readers fascinated by Anne Frank's diary will also appreciate these survival stories.(Grades 7+)

Strom, Yale. *A Tree Still Stands: Jewish Youth in Eastern Europe Today.* New York: Philomel, 1990.

The author toured Eastern Europe just before German reunification, as countries like Czechoslovakia and Romania were beginning to deal with their independence. His photos and interviews with Jewish young people, some of the 200,000 Jews remaining in Eastern Europe today, are a powerful and poignant reminder of the lasting effects of the Holocaust. (Grades 5-8)

Takashima, Shizuye. *A Child in Prison Camp.* Montreal: Tundra, 1971.

Writing in diary form, the author has recreated her experiences as a young girl living in an internment camp established by the Canadian government for its Japanese citizens during World War II. The details are childlike and revealing, and the diary format creates an immediacy that contemporary children should be able to relate to. This was named the "Best Illustrated Book of the Year" by the Canadian Association of Children's Librarians for its delicate, poignant watercolor illustrations. (Grades 5-8)

Taylor, Theodore. *Air Raid—Pearl Harbor! The Story of December 7, 1941.* New York: Crowell, 1971; Harcourt Brace Jovanovich, 1991.

The author documents the events in Japan and the United States that preceded the Japanese attack on Pearl Harbor, including the famous coded messages that were kept secret from the American military leaders who might have been able to prepare a defense if they had known about them. The attack itself is described with relentless detail, and some of the immediate consequences are presented. (Grades 6-8)

Teenage Soldiers, Adult Wars. New York: Rosen, 1991.

An anthology of writings and photo-essays by and about the young people who have fought in wars throughout the world in recent years. (Grades 7+)

Tsuchia, Yukio. *Faithful Elephants: A True Story of Animals, People and War.* Illustrated by Ted Lewin. Translated by Tomoko Tsuchiya Dykes. Boston: Houghton Mifflin, 1988.

During World War II, the Japanese army ordered that the wild animals in the Ueno Zoo in Tokyo be killed in order to prevent their escaping as a result of a bomb hit. The keepers reluctantly complied, but the faithful elephants broke their hearts as they continued to perform their tricks even as they starved to death. In spite of the picture book format, this should be saved for older children; readers are not spared the knowledge of the suffering that the animals endured. (Grades 5-8)

Tunis, Edwin. *Weapons: A Pictorial History.* Cleveland: World, 1954.

A thorough history of weapons in the Western world from the Stone Age to the hydrogen bomb. The text is much more extensive than that of Michele Byam's *Arms and Armor*, and the black-and-white drawings add fascinating detail. (Grades 4-8)

Valentine, E.J. *H. Norman Schwarzkopf.* New York: Bantam, 1991.

A flattering biography of the complicated man who commanded Operation Desert Storm. (Grades 5-7)

Weidhorn, Manfred. *Robert E. Lee*. New York: Atheneum, 1988.
> In this adulatory biography the author describes Lee as ". . . a classic example of a decent and honorable man who somehow ends up on the wrong side" (p. 26). In spite of the cloying tone, this is a detailed, interesting account of the life of one of the Civil War figures whose gaze haunts us today from Matthew Brady's famous photographs. (Grades 6-9)

Windrow, Martin. *The Civil War Rifleman*. Illustrated by Jeffrey Burn. New York: Watts, 1985.
> Detailed drawings and a brief text communicate a wealth of detail about Civil War foot soldiers—their uniforms, weapons, daily life, and battle experiences. (Grades 4-6)

————. *The Medieval Knight*. Illustrated by Richard Hook. New York: Watts, 1985.
> This lavishly illustrated book, part of the Soldier Through the Ages series, is a realistic antidote to the romanticism of most children's literature about knights. It includes information on the political system that supported the knights, their training, their weapons, their opponents, and the consequences of the wars in which they fought. (Grades 4-6)

————. *The Roman Legionary*. Illustrated by Gerry Embleton. New York: Watts, 1984.
> This book offers fascinating information about the soldiers who maintained the far-flung Roman Empire. (Grades 4-6)

————. *The Viking Warrior*. Illustrated by Angus McBride. New York: Watts, 1984.
> The usual lavishly illustrated text presents details about the Norse sea wolves, their longships, armor and weapons, and militaristic religion. (Grades 4-6)

————. *The World War II GI*. Illustrated by Kevin Lyles. New York: Watts, 1984.
> In addition to the expected information about uniforms and weapons, European foxholes, and jungle military strategy, there is a section on streptomycin and penicillin, the life-saving wonder drugs that made their appearance during World War II. (Grades 4-6)

Learning about Peace and Conflict Resolution

Stories for Young Children

Cowley, Joy. *The Duck in the Gun*. Illustrated by Edward Sorel. New York: Doubleday, 1969.
> The general has to delay the war because a duck has built her nest in the cannon. While he and his soldiers wait for the eggs to hatch, they discover many reasons to wage peace instead of war. A simple fable for young readers. (Grades 2-4)

De Paola, Tomie. *The Hunter and the Animals*. New York: Holiday House, 1981.

> In this wordless picture book, a hunter falls asleep after failing to find any animals to shoot. The well-hidden animals take his gun but return it to him when he awakes and finds himself alone and frightened in the woods. In gratitude, he breaks his gun; now the hunter and hunted are just friends. (Grades Preschool-2)

————. *The Knight and the Dragon*. New York: Putnam, 1980.

> A knight and a dragon carefully research their traditional roles and then prepare to fight. A medieval cartmobile librarian who is passing by saves the day by providing books that show peaceful uses for their weapons. In the end, the former adversaries become joint operators of the K & D Bar-B-Q. (Grades Preschool-2)

Eco, Umberto. *The Bomb and the General*. Translated by William Weaver. Illustrated by Eugenio Carmi. San Diego: Harcourt Brace Jovanovich, 1989.

> The atoms who have been put into bombs rebel, silently stealing away and hiding in the cellars where the bombs are kept. When the general declares war, for no other reason than that the bombs are getting moldy from disuse and he wants to advance his career, he drops the bombs from his airplane. The bombs do not explode, however, because they are empty (remember the rebellious atoms?), so the happy, relieved people use them for flowerpots, and the general becomes a hotel doorman. A poorly conceived, incoherent anti-war fable. (Grades K-2, or for adult readers)

————. *The Three Astronauts*. Translated by William Weaver. Illustrated by Eugenio Carmi. San Diego: Harcourt Brace Jovanovich, 1989.

> The author is better known for his treatises on semiotics and his adult novel, *The Name of the Rose*. Here he has brought that perspective to a book intended for young children. Russian, Chinese, and American astronauts all land on Mars at the same time and are distracted from their plan to kill the green, six-armed Martian when they all—including the Martian—begin to feel pity for a fallen baby bird. "And so the visitors realized that on Earth, and on the other planets, too, each one has his ways, and it's simply a matter of reaching an understanding." The sophisticated illustrations and didactic, contrived text make this more of a novelty item for fashionable adults than a suitable picture book for children. (Grades Kindergarten-2, or for adult readers)

Emberley, Barbara. *Drummer Hoff*. Illustrated by Ed Emberley. New York: Simon & Schuster, 1967.

> This adaptation of a cumulative folk song could be seen as a glorification of militarism, as seven soldiers carry out the tasks needed to fire a cannon. Indeed, it goes off with a mighty "Kahbahbloom." But turn the page and see that flowers do bloom and birds nest and cobwebs grow on a far more peaceful use of the cannon. A Caldecott medal winner. (Grades Preschool-2)

Fitzhugh, Louise. *Bang Bang You're Dead*. Illustrated by Sandra Scoppet-tone. New York: Harper & Row, 1969.

A group of children learn the difference between make-believe war play and war play for real. Sophisticated black-and-white illustrations which graphically depict the bleeding, wounded children contributed to the controversy that surrounded this book when it was first published. (Grades Kindergarten-3)

Foreman, Michael. *The Two Giants*. New York: Pantheon, 1967.

A quarrel over a pink shell between two friendly giants escalates into a great fight. Years pass, and the giants continue to fight even though they have forgotten why they are enemies. When they confront each other face to face at last, they see that they are both wearing mismatched socks. They remember the happy day at the beach when they had still been friends and had gotten their socks mixed up. Peace and happiness are restored, but they continue to wear mismatched socks—just in case. (Grades Preschool-2)

Kellogg, Steven. *The Island of the Skog*. New York: Dial, 1973.

When their home in a mousehole becomes too cramped and too insecure, the mice set off to find a new home on a peaceful island. The new island home proves to be inhabited by a terrible monster, the Skog. Mice and Skog begin to fight over possession of the island. Fortunately, before things go too far, the Skog is unmasked as a weak little rodent much like the mice, and the two sides agree to live together in peace. (Grades Preschool-2)

Lattimore, Deborah Nourse. *The Flame of Peace: A Tale of the Aztecs*. New York: Harper & Row, 1987.

When Two Flint's father dies in battle, the little Aztec boy decides to seek the Lord Morning Star, the god who could bring peace to his people. He uses his wits and courage to make his way to the Hill of the Star, and Lord Morning Star rewards him with the New Fire of Peace, which he places in the temple of his city, Tenochtitlan. (Grades 2-4)

Lavie, Arlette. *Half a World Away*. Sudbury, MA: Playspaces-International, 1990.

Children in a land of peace and plenty become aware of children suffering under a Purple Cloud half a world away. They urge the grown-ups to help. The grown-ups refuse to get involved until the children threaten a hunger strike and the parents are shamed into action. The people convince government leaders to send help to the stricken land. There are some important concepts of social responsibility in this picture book, but the message may outweigh the execution. (Grades Preschool-2)

Leaf, Munro. *The Story of Ferdinand*. Illustrated by Robert Lawson. New York: Viking, 1936.

An early childhood classic about a young bull who would rather smell the flowers than fight. (Grades Preschool-2)

Lionni, Leo. *The Alphabet Tree*. New York: Pantheon, 1968; Dragonfly, 1990.

An ant tells his friend about a wonderful tree on which every leaf was a letter. The tree is vulnerable in a strong wind, however, until a word bug teaches the letters how to become words. A caterpillar then teaches the tree one last trick—how to make sentences. The tree then forms the sentence: "Peace on earth and goodwill toward all men." The caterpillar is so impressed that he asks the letters to hop on his back. "Where are you taking us?" they ask. "To the President," says the caterpillar. (Grades Preschool-2)

Lobel, Arnold. *Frog and Toad Are Friends*. New York: Harper & Row, 1970.

Heads of state as well as ordinary people living ordinary lives could learn much about strategies for conflict resolution and harmonious relationships from this easy reader about two good friends. (Grades Kindergarten-2)

Naylor, Phyllis Reynolds. *King of the Playground*. Illustrated by Nola Langner Malone. New York: Atheneum, 1991.

A young boy's father helps him develop creative strategies for dealing with the playground bully. (Grades Preschool-2)

Oppenheim, Joanne. *On the Other Side of the River*. Illustrated by Aliki. New York: Watts, 1972.

The villagers on the east side of the river don't get along with those on the west side until a crisis demonstrates the need for cooperation. Mutual need is the motivation for conflict resolution in this simplistic picture story. (Grades Kindergarten-3)

Peet, Bill. *The Pinkish, Purplish, Bluish Egg*. New York: Houghton Mifflin, 1963.

Myrtle the dove adopts an egg which hatches into a baby griffin. The other birds worry that the griffin will be too ferocious to live happily with his peaceful mother, but fortunately, he grows up to be ". . . a peace-loving creature and tame as could be." (Grades Kindergarten-2)

Piatti, Celestino. *The Happy Owls*. New York: Atheneum, 1963.

The proud peacock asks the owls why they are so content, unlike the rest of the barnyard fowl who do nothing but eat and drink and fight. The owls describe their delight with the simple passing of the seasons. The other birds reject this as nonsense and go on preening, stuffing themselves, and quarreling, just as they had before. (Grades Preschool-2)

Scholes, Katherine. *Peace Begins with You*. Illustrated by Robert Ingpen. San Francisco: Sierra Club/Boston: Little, Brown, 1990.

Lyrical, simple language and soft images convey the abstract concept of peace for young children. Strategies, as well as reasons, for resolving conflict in one's personal life and at a global level are also presented. (Grades Kindergarten-2)

Singer, Isaac Bashevis. *Why Noah Chose the Dove*. Illustrated by Eric Carle. Translated by Elizabeth Shub. New York: Farrar, Straus and Giroux, 1974.

> The legend of Noah and the dove is retold for young children with glowing illustrations. (Grades Preschool-2)

Udry, Janice May. *Let's Be Enemies*. Illustrated by Maurice Sendak. New York: Harper, 1961.

> Two little boys who are best friends become enemies for a very short while. All reconciliations should be this easy and this quick! (Grades Preschool-2)

Vigna, Judith. *Nobody Wants a Nuclear War*. Niles, IL: Whitman, 1986.

> A little girl and her brother build a shelter because they are afraid there will be a nuclear war. Their mother tells them how she was afraid of nuclear bombs too when she was a little girl and how adults are working all around the world to prevent a nuclear war from ever happening. The story ends with the children taking steps of their own to promote world peace. They make an anti-war banner, take a picture of it, and mail it to the president. (Grades Kindergarten-2)

Wahl, Jan. *The Animals' Peace Day*. Illustrated by Victoria Chess. New York: Crown, 1970.

> The animals' celebration of peace deteriorates into a brawl. The owl reminds them that keeping the peace is not as easy as planning a feast. (Grades Preschool-2)

Zolotow, Charlotte. *The Quarreling Book*. Illustrated by Arnold Lobel. New York: Harper, 1963.

> In this simple picture book, a quarrel spreads from one person to another in an epidemic of bad feelings. Fortunately, the process is reversed when the family dog fails to reciprocate in kind. Good feelings and friendly relationships prevail at the end. (Grades Preschool-2)

Fiction for Children and Young Adults

Avi. *Nothing But the Truth: A Documentary Novel*. New York: Orchard, 1991.

> Philip Molloy hums along while "The Star-Spangled Banner" is played over the loudspeaker during homeroom. His teacher sends him to the vice principal for breaking the rule that requires students to be respectful and silent while the national anthem is played. He claims he was being patriotic; she claims he was being impudent. The failure to resolve this conflict causes it to escalate and become a crisis that affects everybody involved. (Grades 7-9)

Benson, Bernard. *The Peace Book*. New York: Bantam, 1982.

> The naive hand lettering and stick figure illustrations, as well as the child protagonist and the allegorical form of the narrative, give this the appearance of a children's book, but it might be more appropriately considered a fable for adults. More simple-minded than simple, this book nevertheless launched a phenomenon. It was made into a play, *The Peace Child*, by David Woolcombe and performed in London in 1981. Children have been participating in produc-

tions around the world ever since. The theme is that children can inspire adults to seek peace. The book is probably best used with older children as a springboard to discussion about nuclear weapons and social activism. (Grades 6+)

Bosse, Malcolm J. *Ganesh*. New York: Crowell, 1981.

Jeffrey has grown up in India. When his father dies, he returns to the family home in the United States where his accented English, vegetarianism, and Yoga practice seem out of place. One of the popular boys in school, a serious athlete, befriends him and opens the door to social contacts. When the highway commission threatens to take the house that his great-grandfather built, Jeffrey responds with satyagraha, the method of nonviolent resistance that Gandhi used to help free India from British rule. A group of young people join him in his resistance, and the highway commission backs down. A somewhat implausible plot with a heavy didactic message. (Grades 7-9)

Degens, T. *The Game on Thatcher Island*. New York: Viking, 1977.

Eleven-year-old Harry is flattered when the popular, older boys invite him to a secret war game on Thatcher Island. It all turns ugly, however, when the big boys capture and torture his little sister and visitor from the city. Harry learns that he, too, is capable of cruelty. A thought-provoking novel similar in theme to William Golding's *Lord of the Flies*. (Grades 6-8)

Druon, Maurice. *Tistou of the Green Thumbs*. Translated from the French by Humphrey Hare. Illustrated by Jacqueline Duheme. New York: Scribner's, 1958.

This anti-war fable may be too didactic, too naive, and too precious to appeal to most contemporary readers. The notion that flowers could stop a war lost currency about the time of the Kent State incident. Nonetheless, this is a classic example of a European anti-war novel for children. (Grades 4-6)

Jones, Adrienne. *Long Time Passing*. New York: Harper & Row, 1990.

Jonas Duncan has been raised in the Marine Corps, and his officer father expects that he will follow in the tradition when he is through with high school. When his mother dies in a car accident and his father is sent to Vietnam, Jonas is sent to stay with his mother's cousin in a small town on the coast north of San Francisco. There he falls in love with Auleen, a girl who is a war protestor, and plans to join her in a commune in Berkeley. He abandons his new found anti-war politics, however, when he learns that his father is missing in action. He enlists, hoping to find his father himself. Twenty years later, Jonas and Auleen meet again and see how their lives have changed. While the author tries to present both sides of the divisive debate over the Vietnam War, the plot is forced, the dialogue stilted, and the characters comically stereotypical. This novel adds little to the contemporary young person's understanding of the Vietnam War or the peace movement that accompanied it. (Grades 7-9)

Langton, Jane. *The Fragile Flag*. New York: Harper, 1984; HarperTrophy, 1989.

Georgie, the heroine of Langton's *The Fledgling*, decides to walk to Washington, D.C., to hand deliver her letter to the president, telling him "What the Flag of My Country Means to Me." Her walk turns into a Children's Crusade, as thousands of children join her to protest the president's "Peace Missile." The peace message is strong, as is the theme of empowerment. (Grades 4-6)

Leichman, Seymour. *The Boy Who Could Sing Pictures*. New York: Doubleday, 1968.

In this brief fantasy set in an imaginary war-torn kingdom of long ago, a little boy discovers that he can sing pictures that ease the pain and troubles of the people. When he performs for the king, his song-pictures portray the suffering of the people that is caused by the king's senseless wars. The king sees the error of his ways and sets about restoring peace and prosperity in his land. (Grades 3-5)

McKillip, Patricia A. *The Forgotten Beasts of Eld*. New York: Atheneum, 1974.

In this high fantasy, a wizard is drawn into the world of humans, where love and war are both new experiences for her. At last she faces her inner self and her greatest fears and returns to her retreat in the mountains. Her mythical, mystical beasts lead the warring humans to peace. This is an anti-war fable for young people who take their fantasy straight, unleavened by humor. (Grades 8-10)

Millman, Dan. *Secret of the Peaceful Warrior*. Illustrated by T. Taylor Bruce. Tiburon, CA: Starseed, 1991.

The best-selling New Age author and athletic coach brings his message of self-actualization through courage, hard work, and nonviolent confrontation to children. The plot line is slim, featuring a young boy's efforts to overcome the school bully, and the emphasis is on the didactic message. (Grades 3-5)

Myers, Walter Dean. *Scorpions*. New York: Harper & Row, 1988.

For Jamal, a young boy living in contemporary Harlem, the dilemma about whether to use a gun in a fight leads to a conflict with his best friend Tito. The author suggests no easy answers. (Grades 5-8)

Pirtle, Sarah. *An Outbreak of Peace*. Illustrated by Louise Godchaux et al. Philadelphia: New Society, 1987.

Beginning with an art display that celebrates peace, a group of teenagers in a small New England college town go on to enlist the whole community in declaring an outbreak of peace. This well-meaning, politically correct novel contains much information about peace education, but its slender plot and one-dimensional characters fail to support the heavy weight of didacticism that it carries. The illustrations are by young people. (Grades 7-9)

Smith, Doris Buchanan. *Return to Bitter Creek: A Novel*. New York: Viking, 1986.

Generational conflict is seen through the eyes of a twelve-year-old girl. The conflict is between her mother and grandmother; the grandmother has never forgiven her daughter for an unconventional lifestyle, including raising her child out of wedlock. The reconciliation is slow to come and poignant in its ultimate resolution. (Grades 6-8)

Speare, Elizabeth George. *The Bronze Bow*. Boston: Houghton Mifflin, 1961.

> Daniel is converted from his conviction that only force will free Israel from Roman oppression by the philosophy of peace and love taught by Jesus. (Grades 6-8)

Spinelli, Jerry. *Maniac Magee*. Boston: Little, Brown, 1990.

> The hero of this Newbery winner is a peacemaker *naif*. A legend in his own time, Maniac Magee can run faster than anyone, untie any knot, confront the meanest, baddest kid without backing down, and hit an inside-the-park "frog" home run. This homeless youth looks for roots and love and security wherever he can find them—on the all-white West End of town or the all-black East End. His integrity is innocent and unschooled, and his efforts to eliminate racial conflict and tension around him in the Pennsylvania town where he settles are personal, unmotivated by politics or ideology. Young readers may find this look at the complexities of racial conflict more palatable than a heavy-handed, moralistic approach, while adults may worry about the implicit message that the solution to the problem of racism is beyond the reach of ordinary human beings. (Grades 6-9)

Wahl, Jan. *How the Children Stopped the Wars*. Illustrated by Mitchell Miller. New York: Farrar, Straus and Giroux, 1969.

> Uillaume is a shepherd boy whose mother is dead and whose father has been off to the wars for so long his son has nearly forgotten him. A mysterious stranger conjures up visions of the horrors of those wars, and Uillaume sets off to stop them. Swarms of children join his crusade. When they finally reach the battlefront, the fighting stops simply because the fathers are so happy to see their children again. A wispy fantasy based on wishful thinking rather than political reality. (Grades 4-6)

Wolitzer, Meg. *Caribou*. New York: Greenwillow, 1985.

> While this is a novel about the Vietnam era in the United States, its focus is on anti-war activities. Sixth-grader Becca Silverman lives with the conflict in her family after her brother chooses to go to Canada to avoid the draft. Finally, in support of her brother and in acknowledgment of her own growing anti-war sentiments, she makes a dramatic gesture of her own, turning a mural of a patriotic parade into a picture of an anti-war demonstration. (Grades 6-8)

Nonfiction

Aaseng, Nathan. *The Peace Seekers: The Nobel Peace Prize*. Minneapolis: Lerner, 1987.

> In addition to background about the Nobel Peace Prize, the author presents brief accounts of the work of nine recipients of the prize: Jane Addams, Carl von Ossietzky, Linus Pauling, Martin Luther King, Jr., Andrei Sakharov, Betty Williams and Mairead Corrigan, Lech Walesa, and Desmond Tutu. (Grades 3-6)

Adler, David A. *A Picture Book of Martin Luther King, Jr.* Illustrated by Robert Casilla. New York: Holiday House, 1989.

This biography of the civil rights and peace activist who won the Nobel Peace Prize is for the youngest child. This could be read aloud to a 4-year-old or read independently by a second-grader. (Grades Kindergarten-3)

Armstrong, Louise. *How to Turn War into Peace: A Child's Guide to Conflict Resolution.* Illustrated by Bill Basso. New York: Harcourt Brace Jovanovich, 1979.

Using the example of two children fighting over their sand castles, the author demonstrates the terminology and concepts of international diplomacy. (Grades 2-4)

Ashabranner, Brent. *Gavriel and Jemal: Two Boys of Jerusalem.* Photographs by Paul Conklin. New York: Dodd, Mead, 1984.

In this even-handed account of the lives of a young Israeli boy and a young Palestinian Arab boy and their families, the author makes it clear that only they and others of their generation have any hope of solving the conflicts between Arabs and Jews in the Middle East. "The voices of violence and bitter enmity surround them, and they, like all other young Palestinians and Israelis, are ground between the millstones of prejudice and fear . . . . The disease of hate has not yet blighted these two boys of Jerusalem, and perhaps it never will" (p. 88). (Grades 5-8)

Bush, Catherine. *Gandhi.* New York: Chelsea House, 1985.

A political biography of the man who brought India to independence, using the philosophy and tactics of nonviolence. (Grades 6-9)

Celsi, Teresa. *Rosa Parks and the Montgomery Bus Boycott.* Brookfield, CT: Millbrook, 1991.

In addition to the biographical information about Rosa Parks and the story of the Montgomery bus boycott, there are sidebars here about other issues related to the civil rights movement—segregated schools, the Freedom Train, the use of boycotts in protest movements. While the author does not make explicit that the bus boycott was an act of nonviolent resistance, thoughtful young readers will see how that strategy worked in this instance. (Grades 3-5)

Durrell, Ann, and Marilyn Sachs, editors. *The Big Book for Peace.* New York: Dutton, 1990.

This anthology of poetry, pictures, story, and song is a joyful celebration of peace by some of the finest writers and illustrators for children. This is especially appropriate for family sharing. (All ages)

Fitzgerald, Merni Ingrassia. *The Peace Corps Today.* New York: Dodd, Mead, 1986.

Since the author was employed with the public affairs office of the Peace Corps at the time she wrote this book, it is no surprise that this is a positive, upbeat portrayal of the organization, presented within the framework of 1980s conservatism. Still, this is the most up-to-date book available on the Peace Corps, and it does present both a historical overview as well as the current emphasis of the program. Because of its date of publication, it does not cover the controversial extension of the program into Eastern Europe following the democracy movements in 1990. (Grades 5-7)

Franchere, Ruth. *Cesar Chavez.* Illustrated by Earl Thollander. New York: Harper & Row, 1970; HarperTrophy, 1985.

This simple biography focuses on the boyhood of the man who grew up to lead the farmworkers in their organizing effort. The author does not make explicit Chavez' use of nonviolent resistance as a strategy, but she does show the value of cooperation in the face of injustice. (Grades 2-4)

Fry-Miller, Kathleen, and Judith Myers-Walls. *Young Peacemakers Project Book.* Illustrated by Janet Domer-Shank. Elgin, IL: Brethren Press, 1988.

This collection of activities and projects for children ages three to ten is organized into three sections: "Caring For the Environment," "Understanding People," and "Making Peace." The book could be used independently by children or as a resource for adults working with children. (Grades Preschool-4)

Fry-Miller, Kathleen, Judith Myers-Walls, and Janet Domer-Shank. *Peace Works: Young Peacemakers Project Book II.* Elgin, IL: Brethren Press, 1989.

In their introduction, the authors state: "Peacemaking is more than building a just society and righting wrongs; it is the skill of approaching daily life joyfully and holding a positive attitude toward the future." Building on that premise, this is a more celebratory book than the first volume. There are three sections of activities: "Fun with Nature," "Fun with Toys," and "Fun with People." (Grades Preschool-4)

Habensreit, Barbara. *Men Against War.* New York: Doubleday, 1973.

A history of anti-war and pacifist movements in the United States. In spite of what the unfortunate title might suggest, the book includes information about women pacifists as well as men. (Grades 6-9)

Hakim, Rita. *Martin Luther King, Jr. and the March Toward Freedom.* Brookfield, CT: Millbrook, 1991.

The author spells out Gandhi's influence on King's philosophy of nonviolent resistance. The emphasis of this book is political, not biographical, showing how Martin Luther King shaped the civil rights movements of the 1960s. (Grades 3-5)

Jampolsky, Gerald G., editor. *Children as Teachers of Peace.* Berkeley, CA: Celestial Arts, 1982.

An anthology of drawings, essays, and poems by children which complete the statement "Peace is . . . ". The children seem to have more understanding of the political and social forces that create wars than do the New Age adults involved with this book. (Grades 4-6)

Lewis, Barbara A. *The Kid's Guide to Social Action: How to Solve the Social Problems You Choose—And Turn Creative Thinking into Positive Action*. Minneapolis: Free Spirit, 1991.

> A terrific, practical manual for children who want to make a difference in the political process. (Grades 4-8)

Meltzer, Milton. *Ain't Gonna Study War No More: The Story of America's Peace Seekers*. New York: Harper & Row, 1985.

> This is a particularly informative and readable history of pacifism in the United States. It sheds light on both war and peace as they have been perceived and experienced in this country. (Grades 6-9)

Moore, Melinda, and Laurie Olson. *Our Future at Stake: A Teenager's Guide to Stopping the Nuclear Arms Race*. Philadelphia: New Society, 1985.

> Looking back from our perspective in the post-Cold War 1990s, it may appear that the nuclear arms race has been significantly slowed, if not stopped. Many young people have turned to the threat of ecological disaster as a focus point instead. Nuclear and peace activists, however, have not relaxed their vigilance or eased their concerns. This source book is packed with information about the techniques of social activism as well as nuclear weapons and the threat of nuclear war. (Grades 7-12)

My World/Peace: Thoughts and Illustrations from the Children of All Nations. Lincolnwood, IL: Passport Books, 1985.

> A sample of the quotes from children that are included in this book is one from Mpeo Seroto, a thirteen-year-old child from Lesotho: "I would like my children to live in a calm country with peace. The country free from quarrels, the country where everybody feels free, the country where wanderers may get shelter." (Grades 4-6)

Schechter, Betty. *The Peaceable Revolution: The Story of Nonviolent Resistance*. Boston: Houghton Mifflin, 1963.

> A readable discussion of the nonviolent resistance practiced by Henry Thoreau, Mohandas Gandhi, and participants in the early years of the Civil Rights movement in the American South. (Grades 6-10)

Twain, Mark. *The War Prayer*. Illustrated by John Groth. New York: Harper & Row, 1970.

> Mark Twain asked that this passionate plea for peace not be published until after his death. (Grades 7+)

Timeless Truths from Folk and Fairy Tales

Babbitt, Ellen C. *The Jatakas: Animal Stories*. Illustrated by Ellsworth Young. New York: Appleton-Century-Crofts, 1940.

> These Indian Buddhist tales are all moral stories. Two that are particularly relevant to the teaching of peace are "The Banyan Deer," which has a strong

message about self-sacrifice, and "The Elephant Girly Face," in which a gentle elephant is taught to be cruel by brutal humans. (Grades 3-6)

Brown, Marcia. *Once a Mouse...* New York: Macmillan, 1961.

In this picture book version of a fable from India, a hermit with magical powers changes a mouse into a cat, a dog, and finally a tiger. In the process, he learns much about the vanity of large creatures who truly come to believe that might is right. (Grades Kindergarten-3)

————. *Stone Soup.* New York: Scribner, 1947.

Three soldiers are on their way home from the wars. French villagers see them coming and hide their food because they know that soldiers are always hungry. The soldiers offer to teach them how to make stone soup, and the villagers are gently tricked into sharing their food. The soldiers are more than con men, however; in return for the food, they give the villagers an opportunity for feasting. (Grades Kindergarten-4)

Bruchac, Joseph. "Loo-Wit, the Fire-Keeper," in *Native American Stories.* Illustrated by John Kahionhes Fadden. Golden, CO: Fulcrum, 1991.

In this tale from the Nisqually people of the Pacific Northwest, a beautiful woman named Loo-Wit is turned into the mountain now known as Mount Saint Helens. Two quarreling chiefs became the mountains on either side of her. As custodian of a great fire, she is able to demonstrate her displeasure with the wars of humans and their disrespect for the land. "So they said long before the day in the 1980s when Mount St. Helens awoke again" (p. 25). (Grades 4-6)

Courlander, Harold. *The Tiger's Whisker and Other Tales and Legends from Asia and the Pacific.* Illustrated by Enrico Arno. New York: Harcourt, Brace, 1959.

In "The Spear and Shield of Huan-Tan," a Chinese story, the foolishness of war is symbolized by the weapons maker's boast that he has made a shield that can't be penetrated by any spear and a spear that can penetrate anything. "The Prince of the Six Weapons," an Indian story, tells how the young prince learns that the bow, the spear, the shield, the war-ax, and the sword are nothing without the sixth weapon, knowledge. (Grades 4-6)

Courlander, Harold, and Wolf Leslau. *The Fire on the Mountain and Other Ethiopian Stories.* Illustrated by Robert W. Kane. New York: Holt, 1950.

This collection contains several stories which reflect human responses to war and its causes. "The Battle of Eghal Shillet" is a Somali tale about the clever strategies one man used to avoid going to war. "The Goats Who Killed the Leopard," a story from Eritrea, explains why a man who is wronged by someone stronger than himself often avenges himself on someone who is weaker. "The Messenger Donkey" is a reminder that all living creatures long for liberty. (Grades 4-6)

Finger, Charles J. *Tales from Silver Lands.* Illustrated by Paul Honore. New York: Doubleday, 1925.

These stories from Latin America reflect values, customs, and beliefs from both the indigenous people and their European conquerors. "Na-Ha the Fighter" could be read as an allegory of the conquest. "The Four Hundred" is a story about the exploits of a warrior band, equipped with silver helmets and shields and an unbroken fellowship. "The Tale of the Gentle Folk" tells about a gentle people who were turned into a herd of huanacos rather than submit to conquest by evil men. (Grades 5-8)

Grimm, Wilhelm. *Dear Mili*. Illustrated by Maurice Sendak. Translated from the German by Ralph Manheim. New York: Farrar, Straus & Giroux, 1988.

While this is more likely an original fairy tale rather than one of the folktales collected by the Grimm brothers, it has the structure of a folktale along with the trappings of a religious allegory. A mother sends her daughter into the forest to save her from a war which is ravaging the country. Saint Joseph protects the child for three days and then sends her back to her mother. Thirty years have passed outside of the forest, and mother and child die after their joyful reunion. The Sendak illustrations add another dimension to the story, with visual allusions to the Holocaust. While the combination of Grimm and Sendak would seem to be magical, it is in fact difficult to imagine the child reader who would respond to this obscure and didactic book. Its best audience is probably adult fans of Sendak's illustration art. Some parents may find it a suitable read-aloud for their children; it would require some adult mediation. (Grades 3-5, or adults)

Hamilton, Virginia. *In the Beginning: Creation Stories from Around the World*. Illustrated by Barry Moser. San Diego: Harcourt Brace Jovanovich, 1988.

While these creation myths do not speak directly to issues of peace or war, taken together they are a powerful statement of both the universality of the human condition and the yearning for understanding that underlies all philosophies and religions. As such, it makes a strong foundation for teaching peace. (Grades 6+)

————. *The People Could Fly: American Black Folktales*. Illustrated by Leo and Diane Dillon. New York: Knopf, 1985.

These stories, with their roots in Africa, sustained American black people during slavery. They passed on the lore and wisdom that facilitated survival and nourished the longing for freedom that kept hope alive for a captive people. They were a form of nonviolent resistance. (Grades 5-8)

Kismaric, Carole. *The Rumor of Pavel and Paali*. Illustrated by Charles Mikolaycak. New York: Harper & Row, 1988.

One brother is kind and generous; the other is cruel and selfish. At first, it seems as though the evil brother will triumph, but in the end, the folly of selfish, vicious greediness is demonstrated in this Ukrainian folktale. (Grades 2-4)

MacDonald, Margaret Read. *Look Back and See: Twenty Lively Tales for Gentle Tellers*. Illustrated by Roxane Murphy. New York: H.W. Wilson, 1991.

With this collection, the well-known storyteller and folklorist responds to requests for tellable tales with less violence than is found in so much of the standard storytelling repertoire. Many of these stories also have a moral or message which encourages nonviolence or creative conflict resolution. "Grandfather Bear Is Hungry" and "The Singing Turtle" show the rewards of being kind, for example, while "Turkey Girl" demonstrates the consequences of failing to meet one's social responsibilities. (For adults to share with children of all ages.)

Moser, Barry. *The Tinderbox*. Boston: Little, Brown, 1990.

The author/illustrator/adaptor of Hans Christian Andersen's story has placed it in the context of the post-Civil War South. The hero is a Confederate soldier returning to his home in the Tennessee mountains. The watercolor illustrations evoke the period, and the text makes us see the soldier's motivation. Other editions of this story depict a more generic soldier; this one is clearly a veteran of a particular war. (Grades 4-6)

Rockwell, Anne. *The Emperor's New Clothes*. New York: Crowell, 1982.

This retelling of the classic Hans Christian Andersen tale retains the essence of the original while adding a modern flavor. The message is still relevant and applicable to contemporary rulers and public policy as well. (Grades Kindergarten-4)

Wolkstein, Diane. *The Magic Orange Tree and Other Haitian Folktales*. Illustrated by Elsa Henriquez. New York: Schocken, 1978.

The most relevant story in this fine collection is "I'm Tippingee, She's Tipingee, We're Tipingee, Too." School girls protect their friend, who is in danger of being sold to an old man by her selfish stepmother, by dressing like her and even claiming to be her when he comes looking. The storyteller Nancy Schimmel compares this to the behavior of the Danish gentiles who put on yellow stars when their Jewish neighbors were ordered to wear them. (Grades 4-8)

Yolen, Jane. *The Girl Who Cried Flowers and Other Tales*. Illustrated by David Palladini. New York: Crowell, 1974.

These are haunting original fairy tales. "Silent Bianca" is the bittersweet story about how a young women outwitted an army and won a kingdom. (Grades 5-8)

The Vision of Poets

Cole, William, editor. *I'm Mad at You*. Illustrated by George MacClain. New York: Collins, 1978.

This collection of poems for young children emphasizes the comic aspects of anger and consequently may seem a poor choice to add to one's understanding of either war or peace. However, some of these poems might be used by an adult to introduce more serious treatments of anger and its consequences; and some, such as the selection by Myra Cohn Livingston, suggest a universe of meaning in a few short lines. (Grades Kindergarten-4)

Eliot, T.S. *Growltiger's Last Stand and Other Poems*. Illustrated by Errol Le Cain. New York: Farrar Straus Giroux/Harcourt Brace Jovanovich, 1987.

These selections from Eliot's *Old Possum's Book of Practical Cats* have been criticized by some adults as being too violent to be shared with children. Indeed, the encounter between the old fighter Growltiger and the Siamese cats, who are well-armed with toasting forks and carving knives, is a battle to the death. The insurrection of the ordinarily peaceful Pekes and Pollicles is played entirely for laughs, however, and the pampered puppies scatter like sheep after just one threatening leap from the great Rumpuscat. And after the wars come the rewards of peace, represented here by the irresistible, pleasure-seeking Jellicle Cats. (Grades 2+)

Harrison, Michael, and Christopher Stuart-Clark, eds. *Peace and War: A Collection of Poems*. Illustrated by Alan Marks. Oxford: Oxford University Press, 1989.

A rich selection of poetry in an accessible format. While the emphasis is on English-speaking poets, other voices are also represented. (Grades 7+)

Longfellow, Henry Wadsworth. *Paul Revere's Ride*. Illustrated by Nancy Winslow Parker. New York: Greenwillow, 1985.

Illustrations, notes, and a glossary add to the historical context of the famous poem. (Grades 4-6)

Volavkova, Hana, editor. *I Never Saw Another Butterfly: Children's Drawings and Poems, Terezin 1942-1944*. Translated by Jeanne Nemcova. New York: Schocken, 1978.

Terezin, in Czechoslovakia, was intended by the Nazis to be their "model camp," one that they could show foreign delegations such as the Red Cross as an example of their humane treatment of the Jews they had imprisoned. In reality, it was a way station for the extermination camps such as Auschwitz, and out of 15,000 children who entered Terezin between the years of 1942 and 1944, only 100 survived. While they were there, adults taught them secretly; and the poems and drawings in this collection are artifacts of that clandestine schooling. They will break your heart. (Grades 6+)

Whittier, John Greenleaf. *Barbara Frietchie*. Illustrated by Paul Galdone. New York: Crowell, 1965.

Whittier, an ardent abolitionist, wrote this poem to commemorate an actual incident in which an old woman waved the Union flag in defiance of Stonewall Jackson as he rode with his Confederate troops through her town of Frederick, Maryland. This is patriotic doggerel of more historical than literary merit, once memorized by American school children: "'Shoot, if you must, this old gray head/But spare your country's flag,' she said." (Grades 4+)

Resources for Adults

War and Peace

Capa, Cornell, and Richard Whelan, editors. *Children of War, Children of Peace: Photographs by Robert Capa*. Boston: Bulfinch/Little, Brown, 1991.

> This beautifully presented collection by the famous war photographer should remind all adults about the impact that war has on children. The black-and-white photographs are breathtakingly beautiful and heartbreakingly poignant.

David, Kati. *A Child's War: World War II Through the Eyes of Children*. New York: Avon, 1989.

> The author, who was herself a Jewish child in Amsterdam and Budapest during World War II, has interviewed other adults from different European countries about their childhood memories of World War II. From these interviews, she has constructed 15 memoirs of a war dimly understood but vividly remembered. Although this book was intended for adults, many young readers would also find it meaningful.

Dwork, Deborah. *Children with a Star: Jewish Youth in Nazi Europe*. New Haven: Yale University Press, 1991.

> The author uses historical documents and oral histories to reconstruct the nature of childhood for Jewish children in the European countries controlled by the Nazis. This perspective has been curiously lacking and is essential to truly understanding the Holocaust. This book looks at the most vulnerable members of the persecuted Jewish community, elucidating clearly how the Nazi strategies progressed and how Jews and gentiles responded.

Eisen, George. *Children and Play in the Holocaust: Games among the Shadows*. Amherst, MA: University of Massachusetts Press, 1988.

> The author has applied the psychological research on children's play to the phenomenon of children's play in the ghettos and death camps of the Holocaust, as recorded in many historical documents. His analysis stops short of deep insight—one senses that this book was as painful to write as it is to read—but provides a necessary accounting of the role that Jewish children played for the adults in their communities as well as to the Germans who annihilated them.

Elshtain, Jean Bethke. *Women and War*. New York: Basic Books, 1987.

> A prominent political theorist takes both a personal and a scholarly look at the roles women have played as warriors and peacemakers.

Feldbaum, Carl B., and Ronald J. Bee. *Looking the Tiger in the Eye: Confronting the Nuclear Threat*. New York: Harper & Row, 1988.

> This readable, objective history of the development of nuclear weapons and their effect on foreign policy includes a plea for informed citizen participation in the decisions that democratic governments make.

Garbarino, James, Kathleen Kostelny, and Nancy Dubrow. *No Place to Be a Child: Growing Up in a War Zone.* Lexington, MA: Lexington, 1991.

The authors, all researchers in child development at the Erikson Insitute in Chicago, document the lives of children living in the violence and chaos of contemporary Cambodia, Mozambique, Nicaragua, the West Bank, and south-side Chicago.

LaFarge, Phyllis. *The Strangelove Legacy: Children, Parents, and Teachers in the Nuclear Age.* New York: Harper & Row, 1987.

A former editor of *Parents* magazine presents a far-reaching discussion on the significance of the nuclear threat in the lives of children and youth.

McCloud, Bill. *What Should We Tell Our Children About Vietnam?* Norman, OK: University of Oklahoma Press, 1989.

A compilation of letters from a variety of people, both famous and unknown, to a junior high social studies class, all answering the question posed by the title. The author/editor was the teacher who solicited the letters; he offers his own insights on teaching contemporary children about the Vietnam War.

Rosenblatt, Roger. *Children of War.* New York: Anchor/Doubleday, 1983.

This is a journalist's account of the lives of children in war-torn Belfast, Israel, Lebanon, Cambodia, and Vietnam. Rosenblatt shares his admiration for the resiliency of children whom war has robbed of their childhood.

Parenting, Teaching, Guiding

Carlsson-Paige, Nancy, and Diane E. Levin. *"The Butter Battle Book*: Uses and Abuses with Young Children," *Young Children*, Vol. 41, No. 3 (March, 1986), pp. 37-42.

A good discussion of appropriate nursery school uses of the book in which Dr. Seuss metaphorically portrays the nuclear arms race.

Carlsson-Paige, Nancy, and Diane E. Levin. *The War Play Dilemma: Balancing Needs and Values in the Early Childhood Classroom.* New York: Teachers College Press, 1987.

The issue of war play in the preschool environment is treated with common sense and sensitivity. This is a more middle-of-the-road approach than their later book, *Who's Calling the Shots? How to Respond Effectively to Children's Fascination with War Play and War Toys.*

Carlsson-Paige, Nancy, and Diane E. Levin. *Who's Calling the Shots? How to Respond Effectively to Children's Fascination with War Play and War Toys.* Philadelphia: New Society, 1990.

In this discussion of war toys and war play, two early childhood education specialists explain why they are taking a stronger stand against aggressive play than they did in their earlier book and give practical suggestions for other parents and educators.

Cloud, Kate et al. *Watermelons Not War: A Support Book for Parenting in the Nuclear Age*. Philadelphia: New Society, 1984.

> This is a resource book for parents who want reassurance as well as guidance in raising their children positively and peacefully in a militaristic society in a nuclear age.

Dorn, Lois. *Peace in the Family: A Workbook of Ideas and Actions*. New York: Pantheon, 1983.

> Growing out of the Society of Friends' program for giving support to families, this is a guide for parents who want to incorporate principles of peace, cooperation, and nonviolence into their family life.

Drew, Naomi. *Learning the Skills of Peacemaking: An Activity Guide for Elementary-Age Children on Communicating, Cooperating, Resolving Conflict*. Rolling Hills Estates, CA: Jalmar, 1987.

> An elementary school teacher provides 56 lesson plans that teach the skills of peacemaking in three stages: "Peace Begins with Me," "Integrating Peacemaking into Our Lives," and "Exploring Our Roots and Interconnectedness."

Hall, Mary Bowen, and Sue Mansfield. *Why Are There Wars? Powerful Ideas for Teaching Writing Skills*. Glenview, IL: Scott, Foresman, 1986.

> Hall has adapted Mansfield's historical and psychological theories about the origins of war and created a writing curriculum for grades five to eight.

Judson, Stephanie. *A Manual on Nonviolence and Children*. Philadelphia: New Society, 1984.

> This is a guide for teachers on how to teach the skills of nonviolent conflict resolution in the classroom. Includes a large section of cooperative games for children and adults.

McGinnis, James, editor. *Partners in Peacemaking: Family Workshop Models Guidebook for Leaders*. St. Louis: Parenting for Peace and Justice, 1984.

> This is a detailed manual for conducting peace education workshops for families in a variety of settings, including churches and family camps. It assumes some knowledge of basic peace and conflict resolution models.

McGinnis, Kathleen, and James McGinnis. *Parenting for Peace and Justice*. Maryknoll, NY: Orbis, 1985.

> Two Christian parents share their philosophy and practices for integrating their social ministry and their family ministry. Topics include nonviolence, multicultural awareness, sex-role stereotyping, and family involvement in social action.

Prokop, Michael S. *Kids Coping with War: How Young People React to Military Conflict*. Illustrated by Dennis J. McCullough and young artists. Warren, OH: Alegra House, 1991.

> Although no specific war is mentioned in this workbook for young people, this was clearly intended as a therapeutic tool to use with American children affected by the Persian Gulf War, particularly those with parents serving in the armed forces.

Reardon, Betty A., editor. *Educating for Global Responsibility: Teacher-Designed Curricula for Peace Education*. New York: Teachers College Press, 1988.

    This collection of classroom teaching ideas and lesson plans demonstrates how to integrate peace education into all areas of the curriculum at all grade levels, from K-12. The learning goals of peace education are defined here as the development of a set of human capacities—care, concern, and commitment—that are required for the exercise of global responsibility. The conceptual content is broad, covering topics such as multicultural understanding, social responsibility, and the global environment as well as war, peace, and conflict resolution.

Roskies, Diane K. *Teaching the Holocaust to Children: A Review and Bibliography*. KTAV Publishing, 1975.

    Although the author's references to specific children's books are dated now, she has much to say that is helpful about teaching the Holocaust to children in a variety of settings, including both Jewish schools and public schools. Her content analysis of 18 books for children is useful for providing criteria for evaluating literature about the Holocaust.

Spock, Benjamin. *Raising Children in Difficult Times: A Philosophy of Leadership and High Ideals*. New York: Norton, 1974.

    The wise baby doctor's good advice is still reassuring today. In one particularly relevant chapter, he writes about the need to control aggression. While conceding that most six- to twelve-year- old boys play war games and that for most of them it is a means of controlling aggression, he encourages parents to guide their sons away from violent games. He explains, "If I had a three- or four-year-old son who asked me to buy him a pistol, I'd tell him—with a friendly smile, not a scowl—that I didn't want to give him a gun for even pretend shooting because there is too much meanness and killing in the world; that we must all learn how to get along in a friendly way together. I'd ask him if he didn't want some other present instead" (p. 128).

Van Ornum, William, and Mary Wicker Van Ornum. *Talking to Children About Nuclear War*. New York: Continuum, 1984.

    A clinical psychologist and an educational journalist present techniques for talking to children about both the facts of nuclear war and the feelings that it arouses.

Wichert, Suzanne. *Keeping the Peace: Practicing Cooperation and Conflict Resolution with Preschoolers*. Philadelphia: New Society Publishers, 1989.

    Basing her approach on five years of experience in a preschool/day care whose objectives included an active interpretation of humanistic values and the integration of age-relevant conflict resolution practices into the program, the author provides considerable insight and practical advice for both early childhood educators and parents of young children. She provides step-by-step approaches to negotiating and communicating with preschoolers. In addition to detailing her reasons for limiting war play, she provides specific alternate adventure play ideas. The final section is a compendium of activities for groups of young children which encourage cooperative task completion, improve communication skills, develop self esteem, and foster altruistic behavior.

Children's Literature

Bacon, Betty, editor. *How Much Truth Do We Tell the Children? The Politics of Children's Literature.* Minneapolis: MEP, 1988.
>This collection of essays presents children's literature as a mirror of the dominant social order, expressing prevailing norms and values. Most of the authors are critical of that perspective, advocating a more liberal or progressive world view in books for children. The essays which most directly relate to the topic of war and peace are those by Joel Taxel on issues of race and class in children's books about the American Revolution, by Ursula Sherman on books about the Holocaust, and by Donnarae MacCann on the subject of militarism in children's literature.

Bosmajian, Hamida. "The Anvil or the Crucible? Narrations of Youthful Experiences in Nazi Germany." *The Lion and the Unicorn*, Vol. 15, No. 1 (June, 1991), 59-77.
>The author discusses Max von der Grun's *Howl Like the Wolves* and Barbara Gehrts' *Don't Say a Word*, showing how either the historian's anvil or the novelist's crucible offers only a limited view of human experience.

———. "Conventions of Image and Form in Nuclear War Narratives for Young Readers." *Papers on Language and Literature*, Vol. 27, No. 2 (Winter, 1990), 73-89.
>This scholarly discussion of several young adult novels with nuclear themes focuses on narrative structures which authors have used to present nuclear war to young readers.

———. "Narrative Voice in Young Readers' Fictions About Nazism, the Holocaust, and Nuclear War." In Charlotte F. Otten and Gary D. Schmidt, editors. *The Voice of the Narrator in Children's Literature.* New York: Greenwood, 1989.
>The author deals with the narrative difficulties of presenting children with stories about unthinkable evil while retaining an ultimate message of hope.

Butler, Francelia. "The Theme of Peace in Children's Literature." *The Lion and the Unicorn*, Vol. 14 (1990), 128-38.
>A discussion of peace and conflict resolution in books for children. The author includes a bibliography of children's books that promote peace.

Cadogan, Mary, and Patricia Craig. *Women and Children First: The Fiction of Two World Wars.* London: Gollancz, 1978.
>A readable, scholarly interpretation of British literature produced during the period covering World War I and World War II. The chapters relating to British children's fiction are particularly insightful.

Egoff, Sheila A. *Worlds Within: Children's Fantasy from the Middle Ages to Today*. Chicago: American Library Association, 1988.

> The chapter "Playing in the Shadows of War: Fantasy from the 1940's" shows how World War II influenced writers of fantasy for children.

Eiss, Harry. *Literature for Young People on War and Peace: An Annotated Bibliography*. New York: Greenwood, 1989.

> An annotated, alphabetical listing of 383 titles for children and young adults, as well as a few references for adults.

Farish, Terry. "If You Knew Him, Please Write Me: Novels About the War in Vietnam." *School Library Journal*, Vol. 35, No. 3 (November, 1988), 52-53.

> A children's librarian who served a year as a Red Cross worker in Vietnam during the war discusses some novels that provide clues for today's young people about that war and what it meant to people who experienced it.

Fassler, Joan, and Marjorie Graham Janis. "Books, Children, and Peace." *Young Children*, Vol. 38, No. 6 (September, 1983), 21-30.

> Two specialists in early childhood education suggest ways to use books with young children to encourage them to seek peaceful solutions to problems.

Frew, Andrew W. *"Park's Quest* by Katherine Paterson." *Book Links*, Vol. l, No. 1 (September, 1991), 29-32.

> A reading teacher shares strategies for building classroom activities based on a reading of *Park's Quest*. Additional suggestions for books about family issues, wars and families, Southeast Asia, and the Vietnam War are included.

"Hearts, Minds, and Body Counts: The Vietnam War." *Booklist*, Vol. 86, No. 2 (September 15, 1989), 165-68.

> An excellent annotated bibliography of fiction and nonfiction for young adults.

Kamanetsky, Christa. *Children's Literature in Hitler's Germany: The Cultural Policy of National Socialism*. Athens, OH: Ohio University Press, 1984.

> A scholarly account and analysis of the ideological uses of children's literature as an agent of socialization during the Nazi regime.

Kingston, Carolyn T. *The Tragic Mode in Children's Literature*. New York: Teachers College Press, 1974.

> In Chapter V, the author explores the tragic moment of war as on occasion for heroism in several novels for children. She finds that war tends to create opportunities for heroism and heightened action.

Kleinburd, Freda. "Historical Accuracy in Children's Literature of the Holocaust." *Judaica Librarianship*, Vol. 5, No. 1 (Spring 1989-Winter 1990), 57-61, 70.

> The author discusses the way in which the Holocaust has been treated in a number of books for children. Among the topics she covers are the portrayal of the fate of the Jews in various European countries, the portrayal of Jewish resistance, and the portrayal of non-Jews. She concludes that, considered individually, these novels for children have some flaws or historical inaccura-

cies, but that overall, they present a broad picture of Holocaust events. She also recommends that adults incorporate children's nonfiction about the Holocaust into the curriculum, as well as fiction.

Lenz, Millicent. *Nuclear Age Literature for Youth: The Quest for a Life-Affirming Ethic*. Chicago: American Library Association, 1990.

In this wide-ranging scholarly treatment of nuclear themes in literature for young people, the author focuses on the problem of defining heroism meaningfully in a post-nuclear age. She advocates a more feminine and holistic ethic, exemplified by the Gaia myth.

MacCann, Donnarae. "Militarism in Juvenile Fiction." *Interracial Books for Children Bulletin*, Vol. 13, Nos. 6 & 7 (1982), 18-20.

A brief critical and historical overview of children's fiction about war.

Meir, Rachel. "Introducing Holocaust Literature to Children," *Judaica Librarianship*, Vol. 3, Nos. 1 & 2 (1986-1987), 65-67.

The author points out the difficulties of dealing with the Holocaust experience in literature for children; it is not by its nature the kind of subject considered suitable story material for children. She tells how, nonetheless, books — introduced by sensitive, caring adults — can help children deal with the unthinkable horror of that period.

Paterson, Katherine. "Daughters of Hope." *The Horn Book Magazine*, Vol. 68, No. 2 (March/April, 1992), 164-70.

The author gives counsel and courage to adults who have the responsibility and privilege of working with children in troubled times. She finds reason to be hopeful and cites Saint Augustine, who said that hope has two daughters, anger and courage.

———. "Living in a Peaceful World." *The Horn Book Magazine*, Vol. 67, No. 1 (January/February, 1991), 32-38.

A noted author for children discusses books that promote peace in an essay that inspires and informs.

Polese, Carolyn. "War Through Children's Eyes." *School Library Journal*, Vol. 37, No. 4 (April, 1991), 43-44.

Writing about children's responses to the Persian Gulf War, the author shows how children's books written about childhood experiences during other wars of the twentieth century can help children understand a war that is happening now.

Posner, Marcia W. "Echoes of the Shoa: Holocaust Literature—Part I." *School Library Journal*, Vol. 34, No. 1 (January, 1988), 36-37.

An excellent overview of the issues involved in explaining the Holocaust to children. The author provides a bibliography of resources to help adults help children deal with this subject. She advises that children should not read books about the Holocaust without an adult to share and discuss them.

———. "Echoes of the Shoa: Holocaust Literature—Part II," *School Library Journal*, Vol. 34, No. 2 (February, 1988), pp. 30-31.

In this follow-up to Part I, the author presents a selective, annotated bibliography of books about the Holocaust for children and young adults.

Robb, Laura. *"The Wall* by Eve Bunting." *Book Links*, Vol. 1, No. 1 (September, 1991), 34-36.

> A classroom teacher presents ideas for using *The Wall* with eighth graders. Additional reading suggestions dealing with the Vietnam Memorial and other walls are included.

Sherman, Louise L. "In the Homes of Strangers: The World War II Evacuation of British Children in Children's Literature." *School Library Journal*, Vol. 35, No. 4 (April, 1989), 41-43.

> The author presents a historical survey of novels for children about British evacuees during World War II.

Smith, Charles A. *From Wonder to Wisdom: Using Stories to Help Children Grow*. New York: Plume/New American Library, 1990.

> A specialist in human development writes about using books and stories as a way to help young children deal with such issues as loss, grief, and the consequences of violence.

Stan, Susan. "Peace on Earth." *The Five Owls*, Vol. 5, No. 2 (November/December, 1990), 21-27.

> This article is a discussion of books that can educate children for peace, with a listing of the Jane Addams Children's Book Awards, given annually to a children's book that promotes peace, equality, and social justice.

Taxel, Joel. "The American Revolution in Children's Fiction: An Analysis of Historical Meaning and Narrative Structure." *Curriculum Inquiry*, Vol. 14, No. 1 (1984), 7-55.

> This scholarly analysis treats children's novels about the American Revolution as cultural artifacts of the times in which they were written.

Appendix A: Literature Web for Katherine Paterson's *Park's Quest*

PARK'S QUEST

Vietnam War
Myers. *Fallen Angels*
Kidd. *Onion Tears*
Huynh. *The Land I Lost*
Boyd. *Charlie Pippin*

Black Soldiers
Davis. *Black Heroes of the American Revolution*
Cox. *Undying Glory*
Miller. *Buffalo Soldiers*

Estranged Families
Roberts. *Megan's Island*
Smith. *Return to Bitter Creek*
Voigt. *Dicey's Song*

Divorce
Blume. *It's Not the End of the World*
Cleary. *Dear Mr. Henshawe*

Other Books by Paterson
Of Nightingales That Weep
Rebels of the Heavenly Kingdom

Arthurian Legends
Hastings. *Sir Gawain and the Green Knight*
Pyle. *The Story of the Grail and the Passing of Arthur*
Sutcliff. *Light Beyond the Forest*
Yolen. *The Dragon's Boy*

Aging
Cleaver & Cleaver. *Queen of Hearts*
Hartling. *Old John*
Mahy. *Memory*
Mazer. *A Figure of Speech*

Fathers and Sons
Yep. *Dragonwings*

BOOKS INCLUDED IN THE LITERATURE WEB

Blume, Judy. (1972). It's Not the End of the World. New York: Bradbury.

Boyd, Candy Dawson. (1987). *Charlie Pippin*. New York: Macmillan.

Cleary, Beverly. (1983). *Dear Mr. Henshawe*. New York: Morrow.

Cleaver, Vera, and Bill Cleaver. (1978). *Queen of Hearts*. New York: Lippincott.

Cox, Clinton. (1991). *Undying Glory: The Story of the Massachusetts 54th Regiment*. New York: Scholastic.

Davis, Burke. (1976). *Black Heroes of the American Revolution*. San Diego: Harcourt Brace Jovanovich.

Hartling, Peter. (1990). *Old John*. New York: Lothrop, Lee & Shepard.

Hastings, Selina. (1982). *Sir Gawain and the Green Knight*. New York: Lothrop, Lee & Shepard.

Huynh, Quang Nhuon. (1982). *The Land I Lost: Adventures of a Boy in Vietnam*. New York: Harper & Row.

Kidd, Diana. (1991). *Onion Tears*. New York: Orchard.

Mahy, Margaret. (1987) *Memory*. New York: McElderry/Macmillan.

Mazer, Norma Fox. (1973). *A Figure of Speech*. New York: Delacorte.

Miller, Robert. (1991). *Buffalo Soldiers*. Englewood Cliffs, NJ: Silver Burdett.

Myers, Walter Dean. (1988). *Fallen Angels*. New York: Scholastic.

Paterson, Katherine. (1974). *Of Nightingales That Weep*. New York: Crowell.

———. (1983). *Rebels of the Heavenly Kingdom*. New York: Dutton.

Pyle, Howard. (1985). *The Story of the Grail and the Passing of Arthur*. New York: Scribner.

Roberts, Willo Davis. (1988). *Megan's Island*. New York: Atheneum.

Smith, Doris Buchanan. (1986). *Return to Bitter Creek*. New York: Viking.

Sutcliff, Rosemary. (1980). *The Light Beyond the Forest: The Quest for the Holy Grail*. New York: Dutton.

Voigt, Cynthia. (1982). *Dicey's Song*. New York: Atheneum.

Yep, Laurence. (1975). *Dragonwings*. New York: Harper & Row.

Yolen, Jane. (1990). *The Dragon's Boy*. New York: Harper & Row.

Appendix B: Activity Web for Eleanor Coerr's *Sadako and the Thousand Paper Cranes*

SADAKO AND THE THOUSAND PAPER CRANES

Origami
As a class project, make 1,000
    paper cranes.
Learn to make other origami
    figures.
Araki. *Origami in the Classroom*

**Other Traditional
Japanese Crafts**
Make kites
    Eden. *Kiteworks*
Make paper dolls
    representing traditional
    Japanese festival dolls.
Learn how to do brush painting.

Museum Visit
Compare Japanese and
    Western art.

Learn More About:

**The Bombing of Hiroshima and
Nagasaki**
Lifton. *Return to Hiroshima*
Maruki. *Hiroshima No Pika*
Mattingley. *The Miracle Tree*
Morimoto. *My Hiroshima*

**Efforts to Prevent Another
Nuclear War**
Fry-Miller & Myers-Walls. *Young
    Peacemakers Project Book*
Pringle. *Nuclear War: From
    Hiroshima to Nuclear Winter*

Language Arts
Write a letter to Sadako, telling her
    what you are doing to prevent war.
Read and write haiku poetry.
    Lewis. *In a Spring Garden.*
Write to Japanese pen pals.

BOOKS INCLUDED IN THE ACTIVITY WEB

Araki, Chiyo. (1965-1968). *Origami in the Classroom*. Rutland, VT: Tuttle.

Coerr, Eleanor. (1977). *Sadako and the Thousand Paper Cranes*. New York: Putnam.

Eden, Maxwell. (1989). *Kiteworks: Explorations in Kite Building and Flying*. New York: Sterling.

Fry-Miller, Kathleen, and Judith Myers-Walls. (1988). *Young Peacemakers Project Book*. Elgin, IL: Brethren Press.

Lewis, Richard, editor. (1989). *In a Spring Garden*. New York: Dial.

Lifton, Betty. (1970). *Return to Hiroshima*. New York: Atheneum.

Maruki, Toshi. (1980). *Hiroshima No Pika*. New York: Lothrop.

Mattingley, Christabel. (1985). *The Miracle Tree*. San Diego, Harcourt Brace Jovanovich.

Morimoto, Junko. (1990). *My Hiroshima*. New York: Viking.

Pringle, Laurence. (1985). *Nuclear War: From Hiroshima to Nuclear Winter*. Hillside, NJ: Enslow.

Author Index

This index lists authors of books annotated or mentioned in the Resources section. For authors of children's books mentioned in Chapters 1-3, see the General Index and the list of Children's Books Cited at the end of each chapter.

Title Index

This index lists titles of books annotated or mentioned in the Resources section. For titles of children's books mentioned in Chapters 1-3, see the General Index and the list of Children's Books Cited at the end of each chapter.

Subject Index

This index lists the main subjects and themes of books annotated or mentioned in the Resources section. For topics discussed in Chapters 1-3, see the General Index.

General Index

by Linda Webster

This index lists subjects and children's books mentioned in Chapters 1-3. See also the list of Children's Books Cited at the end of each of those chapters.

3564